SUCCESS WITH READING

10 Easy-to-Read
American History Plays

By Sarah Glasscock

SCHOLASTIC
PROFESSIONAL BOOKS

New York • Toronto • London • Auckland • Sydney
Mexico City • New Delhi • Hong Kong

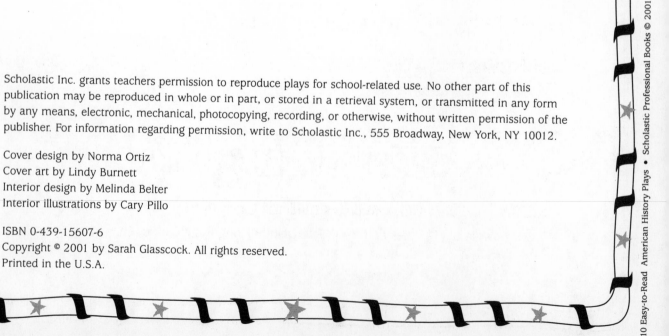

Cover design by Norma Ortiz
Cover art by Lindy Burnett
Interior design by Melinda Belter
Interior illustrations by Cary Pillo

ISBN 0-439-15607-6
Copyright © 2001 by Sarah Glasscock. All rights reserved.
Printed in the U.S.A.

Contents

INTRODUCTION

Purpose

Students at every reading level often complain that learning about history is dull and boring and adds no meaning to their own lives. What we all tend to forget occasionally is that history is going on around us every day. We are a part of history in the making. Your students have experienced a new millennium and are witnesses to a technological revolution. They have lived through the impeachment of a president. History is the story we tell about ourselves, and American history is the story we tell about ourselves and the events that have shaped us as Americans. The aim of these plays is to entertain and inform *all* the readers in your classroom, and to show them that history touches everyone.

How to Use This Book

THE PLAYS can be read aloud or performed in the classroom. Begin by reading the cast of characters and their descriptions aloud to familiarize students with the way each name is pronounced. Encourage everyone to participate; don't let race, ethnicity, or gender determine which student plays a role. Cross-casting gives students an opportunity to view the world in a different way. After assigning the roles, allow enough time for everyone to read the play and become comfortable with the material. Urge students to ask questions about anything they don't understand—or they disagree with. If they think they have a better way to say something, let them experiment with changing the dialog.

Performing the plays can bring in students who are shy or uncertain about performing—especially those who are concerned about their reading ability. These students can be instrumental in designing sets and costumes, directing, creating sound effects, and making programs. Let students suggest places in the plays where non-speaking roles can be enlarged or added. These players can work together to pantomime action when they are onstage.

Above all, students should have fun with the plays. They should make the roles their own whether they're reading at their desks or performing in front of the classroom.

THE TEACHING GUIDE includes a brief background of the events surrounding each play, a list of vocabulary words above a third-grade reading level, a bibliography containing fiction and nonfiction selections, a list of Web sites, and six activities for students.

The **background** provides an overview of the historical events that shaped each play. Review this section, and then share it with students before they read or perform the plays. Although the **vocabulary** lists unfamiliar words and their definitions, you may want to go over each play to determine if any words need to be added to the list. Review the vocabulary with students before they read the plays. Encourage them to mention any words they have trouble understanding. **Books to build interest** contains a wide range of titles for readers aged 9–12. Students with lower reading levels often feel insulted by being given picture books designed for readers aged 4–8. Some of the books in the bibliography may be challenging, so consider pairing or grouping readers with different abilities to study a book or read aloud portions of the book to the class. Two or more **Web sites** (and their host organizations) for each play topic are referenced. Often Web sites offer graphics that can make history really come alive for students. Exploring the content of a variety of Web sites can also help students become more discerning researchers.

After reading each play, assign one or more of the six cross-curricular **activities** to individuals, pairs, or groups of students. A mapping activity is included for each play; suggest that students compile their own map books of American history. As part of the research and report process, encourage them to present their information in fresh and inventive ways. Students shouldn't feel pressured to be creative, but free to report their findings in a way that's exciting and interesting to them. And, since you know your class better than anyone, we urge you to tailor the activities to expand the interests of your students and to meet their needs.

10 Easy-to-Read American History Plays • Scholastic Professional Books © 2001

More Resources

Here is a list of books and Web sites that deal with American history topics:

BOOKS

"The History of U.S." series by Joy Hakim (Oxford University Press)

Biographies of famous Americans by Jean Fritz

"Dear America" series of American-history-based fiction (Scholastic)

Series of books on American exploration edited by William Goetzman (Chelsea House)

Series of books on colonial life by Kate Waters (Scholastic)

"If You Lived…" series exploring American life in previous centuries (Scholastic)

WEB SITES

http://memory.loc.gov/ammem/ammemhome/html (Library of Congress)

http://www/csulb/edu/gc/libarts/am-indian/nae/1600-1750.html (information on Native Americans)

http://www.lib.utexas.edu/Libs/PCL/Map_collection/histus.html (variety of United States historical maps)

COLUMBUS'S MISTAKE

Exploring America (1492)

Cast of Characters (in order of appearance)

Narrator

Paolo Colca: *Italian merchant*

Christopher Columbus: *Italian explorer*

Doña Felipa Perestrello: *Columbus's wife*

Bartholomew Columbus: *Christopher's brother*

Isabella: *Queen of Spain*

Ferdinand: *King of Spain*

Sailors 1–3

Rodrigo de Triana: *Sailor on the* Pinta

Taino Man

Taino Woman

10 Easy-to-Read American History Plays • Scholastic Professional Books © 2001

◄ ACT 1 ►

SCENE 1: A SHOP IN ITALY, 1478

NARRATOR: What was Columbus's mistake? He was sailing to Asia. He didn't know that North and South America were in the way. Nobody in Europe knew the continents were there.

PAOLO COLCA: Christopher Columbus, I hear you're getting married soon. I just got some beautiful silk from China. It would make a fine suit for you to get married in.

CHRISTOPHER COLUMBUS: It is beautiful, but it costs too much.

PAOLO COLCA: What can I do? The cost is high because Asia's a long way off. The roads are so dangerous.

CHRISTOPHER COLUMBUS: It would be safer to travel by sea to Asia.

PAOLO COLCA: Safer? Everybody knows there are monsters in the sea.

CHRISTOPHER COLUMBUS: Not so long ago everybody thought the world was flat. Now we know it's round. There aren't any monsters in the sea.

PAOLO COLCA: I know you make maps. I know you've been a sailor. Tell me—if you know so much, why don't you find a way to sail to Asia?

CHRISTOPHER COLUMBUS: Maybe I will.

SCENE 2: COLUMBUS'S HOUSE IN ITALY, 1483

NARRATOR: Columbus married Doña Felipa Perestrello. Her father had sailed for Prince Henry, the king of Portugal. She gave all of her father's maps to Columbus.

DOÑA FELIPA PERESTRELLO: What do you think, Christopher? Is it possible to sail to Asia?

CHRISTOPHER COLUMBUS: I've looked at your father's maps. I think it's possible. Everybody knows the earth is round, but I think the world is smaller than people say it is. I could sail west from here and reach Asia in less than a month.

BARTHOLOMEW COLUMBUS: In less than a month—are you sure?

CHRISTOPHER COLUMBUS: I think Asia is only 3,000 miles west of us.

BARTHOLOMEW COLUMBUS: But nobody has ever sailed that far west before. You don't know what you might find.

CHRISTOPHER COLUMBUS: I won't ever know if I stay here.

DOÑA FELIPA PERESTRELLO: You'll need ships and men and lots of money for a trip like that. The only people with that much money are kings and queens.

10 Easy-to-Read American History Plays • Scholastic Professional Books © 2001

CHRISTOPHER COLUMBUS: If they give me the money to find a sea route to Asia, they'll be even richer. It'll be safer and quicker and cheaper to bring goods back from China and India and Japan and the East Indies.

DOÑA FELIPA PERESTRELLO: Which king and queen shall we ask first?

CHRISTOPHER COLUMBUS: King John of Portugal.

⬩ ACT 2 ⬩

SCENE 1: THE COURT OF QUEEN ISABELLA AND KING FERDINAND IN SPAIN, 1492

NARRATOR: For a long time, nobody believed Columbus's plan would work. The king of Portugal turned him down. Doña Felipa died. Columbus went to Spain. He asked Isabella and Ferdinand to support his plan. They thought about it for a long time.

ISABELLA: I understand that Portugal turned down your plan, Columbus. Why should we give you money?

FERDINAND: And so much money!

CHRISTOPHER COLUMBUS: Portugal has found an eastern sea route to India.

ISABELLA: Then why do you want to sail west to Asia? Why don't you want to sail around Africa like they're doing?

CHRISTOPHER COLUMBUS: Wouldn't you like Spain to have its own route to Asia? You wouldn't have to worry about Portugal or any other country getting in your way.

FERDINAND: That would mean more money for us!

ISABELLA: Are you sure about this route of yours, Columbus? If you're wrong, we'll lose a lot of money.

CHRISTOPHER COLUMBUS: I'm not wrong.

ISABELLA: Very well. We'll give you ships, money, and a crew.

SCENE 2: ON THE ATLANTIC OCEAN, SEPTEMBER 1492

NARRATOR: On August 3, 1492, Columbus set out with the *Niña*, the *Pinta*, and the *Santa Maria*, and 87 men. Three days later, Columbus had some trouble with the *Niña* and *Pinta*. He spent over a month on the Canary Islands getting the ships fixed.

SAILOR 1: I don't know about this trip. I have a funny feeling about it.

SAILOR 2: Columbus knows what he's doing.

SAILOR 1: How can he know? Nobody's ever sailed this far before.

SAILOR 2: Eat your fish and cheese and stop complaining.

10 Easy-to-Read American History Plays • Scholastic Professional Books © 2001

SAILOR 1: What was that! Did you see that! A fire in the sky!

SAILOR 2: It was a falling star! That's not good. That's not good at all.

SAILOR 1: It's a bad sign, that's what it is. We'll never see Spain or Asia.

➤ ACT 3 ➤

SCENE 1: ON THE ATLANTIC OCEAN, OCTOBER 1492

NARRATOR: The ships got stuck in the Sargasso Sea, which was filled with plants. The sailors grew more and more unhappy. Many of them wanted to turn back. Columbus told the crew that the ships had sailed farther than they really had.

CHRISTOPHER COLUMBUS: We've sailed over 2,500 miles. We'll see land any day now. I want you all to keep your eyes open.

SAILOR 3: All I see is sea and more sea.

CHRISTOPHER COLUMBUS: I'll give the sailor who sees land first a big reward.

(Columbus leaves.)

SAILOR 1: What good is money or gold when there's nowhere to spend it?

SAILOR 2: If we see land, then it's got to be Asia. There'll be plenty of things to buy—silk and spices.

SAILOR 1: How are we going to get back to Spain? The wind will be against us. We'll never be able to sail back.

SAILOR 2: I don't know. I've been thinking about that, too.

SAILOR 3: I've had it. I want to go back home!

SCENE 2: ON BOARD THE *PINTA*, OCTOBER 9, 1492

CHRISTOPHER COLUMBUS: We haven't spotted land yet, but we will soon.

SAILOR 3: I don't believe you. I want to go home!

SAILOR 1: What about the wind? I don't even think we can get back home!

SAILOR 2: Don't forget the shooting star! That's a bad sign.

CHRISTOPHER COLUMBUS: What kind of sailors are you? Are you afraid of a little water and wind?

SAILOR 2: I'm afraid of this water and this wind!

CHRISTOPHER COLUMBUS: All right, I'll tell you what I'll do. If we don't see land in three days, we'll turn back. We'll go back to Spain.

10 Easy-to-Read American History Plays • Scholastic Professional Books © 2001

SAILOR 1: If we can turn back. That wind is blowing against us.

SCENE 3: ON BOARD THE *PINTA*, OCTOBER 12, 1492

RODRIGO DE TRIANA: Look! Look over there! Land! Land ho!

(Columbus rushes in.)

CHRISTOPHER COLUMBUS: Good job, Rodrigo!

SAILOR 1: I knew we could do it.

SAILOR 2: That wasn't so bad. It's only been 33 days since we left the Canary Islands.

SAILOR 3: Rodrigo! Can I borrow some money?

⭐ ACT 4 ⭐

SAN SALVADOR (NOW THE BAHAMAS), OCTOBER 12, 1492

NARRATOR: As you can see, Columbus didn't "discover" the Americas. Native Americans had been here for as long as 20,000 years. The Taino people who lived on the island were friendly to Columbus and his men. Columbus still believed he had reached Asia. Neither the Americans nor the Europeans knew how this meeting would change this part of the world.

CHRISTOPHER COLUMBUS: We've landed on one of the islands of the East Indies. I claim this land for Queen Isabella and King Ferdinand of Spain.

(Columbus plants a Spanish flag in the sand.)

TAINO MAN: What do you think he's doing with that flag?

TAINO WOMAN: Maybe he's sending a signal to his ships.

TAINO MAN: Where do you think they came from?

CHRISTOPHER COLUMBUS *(to the Tainos)*: You must now follow the rules of Spain. Spain will protect you.

TAINO MAN: What is he saying?

TAINO WOMAN: I can't tell. Do you think they're going to stay long?

10 Easy-to-Read American History Plays • Scholastic Professional Books © 2001

TEACHING GUIDE

Background

Many scientists believe that the first people to discover America came from Asia thousands of years ago and were the ancestors of today's Native American peoples. In the tenth century, the Vikings probably sailed to North America and briefly settled there. European exploration, spurred on by Portugal's Prince Henry, began to flourish in the Age of Discovery in the fifteenth century. The riches of the Far East—China, Japan, India, and the East Indies—were shipped to Europe along dangerous land routes, which made the goods expensive. Many European explorers were searching for an eastern sea route to Asia, but Christopher Columbus was convinced that the best route would be to sail to the west.

Despite the advances in science and exploration, Europeans still had an incomplete picture of the world. They knew Earth was a sphere, but none of their maps contained the continents of South and North America. Columbus underestimated Earth's circumference, and he thought that Asia had a much larger land mass than it did. These mistakes led him to conclude that he had reached Asia when he saw the present-day Bahaman Islands.

After years of petitioning the Portuguese and Spanish courts, Columbus was finally able to convince Isabella and Ferdinand of Spain to underwrite his voyage. Outfitted with three ships—the *Niña,* the *Pinta,* and the *Santa Maria*—Columbus left Spain with 87 men on August 3, 1492. On October 12, 1492, he stepped ashore the Taino island, Guanahani, now Watling Island in the Bahamas. He claimed it for Spain, and named it San Salvador. The Taino people living there welcomed Columbus and his crew.

Other Europeans explored various regions of North America. John and Sebastian Cabot arrived in the northeast in 1497; Juan Ponce de León reached present-day Florida in 1513; Giovanni da Verrazzano sailed to North Carolina and then up to Newfoundland in 1524; Hernando de Soto and Francisco Coronado left their marks in the Southeast and Southwest; and Juan Cabrillo explored California in 1542. Exploration continued into the seventeenth century with Bartholomew Gosnold, Samuel de Champlain, Henry Hudson, Louis Jolliet and Jacques Marquette, and Robert La Salle.

Vocabulary Some readers may not be familiar with the following words:

claim: to ask for something that one believes one has a right to

continent: one of seven major land areas on Earth

crew: all the people who work on a ship

dangerous: unsafe

explorer: person who goes to a new place to find out more about it

merchant: person who buys and sells things to make money

Books to Build Interest

If You Were There in 1492 by Barbara Brenner (Aladdin, 1998)

Pedro's Journal by Pamela Conrad (Scholastic, 1992)

Encounter by Jane Yolen (Harcourt Brace, 1992)

Stories from the Days of Christopher Columbus by Richard Young and Judy Dockrey Young (August House, 1992)

Web Site

http://www.mariner.org (The Mariners' Museum Web site)

10 Easy-to-Read American History Plays • Scholastic Professional Books © 2001

ACTIVITIES

Explorers' Awards Show

Students can hold an Explorers' Awards show. Let them nominate explorers who are associated with North America for a variety of different awards such as Best Spanish Explorer, Explorer Who Traveled the Farthest, or Explorer Who Has the Most Places Named for Him, and so on. Individuals, partners, or groups of students can prepare information packets about the explorers to share with the rest of the class. After students have had a chance to look at the material, they can vote for their choice in each category.

Historical Sites

Many explorers have national monuments or sites named after them. For instance, the Cabrillo National Monument is located near San Diego Bay in California, and Hernando de Soto is remembered at the De Soto National Memorial in Bradenton, Florida. Students can find out more about these places by exploring the National Park Service at http://www.nps.gov. Suggest they choose a site to visit. Have them use the Web site's information about location, climate, operating hours and seasons, transportation, and facilities to plan a vacation trip to the national monument or site.

Explorers' Map of America

Groups of students can work together to create a class story map featuring explorers who had an impact in North America. In addition to Columbus, mention the following explorers: Juan Cabrillo, John and Sebastian Cabot, Vasco Nuñez de Balboa, Juan Ponce de León, Giovanni da Verrazzano, Estevan Gómez, Jacques Cartier, Hernando de Soto, Francisco Coronado, Sir Francis Drake, Bartholomew Gosnold, Henry Hudson, Robert La Salle, Samuel de Champlain, and Louis Jolliet and Jacques Marquette.

Time Travel

What would explorers think of North America today? Ask students to imagine that explorers who traveled in this country hundreds of years ago are able to travel through time. The students are in charge of explaining some of the changes to the explorers. What questions do they think the explorers would have? What questions would they like to ask the explorers?

Where Would You Like to Explore?

Explorers had to convince monarchs or companies to give them money and supplies for their expeditions. Pose the following question to students: Where in the world, or the universe, would you like to explore and why? Have them draw up proposals to persuade individuals or institutions to support their expeditions. Encourage students to be creative and convincing.

An Explorer's Life

Students can select an explorer connected with the Americas to immortalize through poetry, song, biography, play, or Web page. Urge them to be critical in examining the impact the explorer had on native peoples and landscapes.

10 Easy-to-Read American History Plays • Scholastic Professional Books © 2001

TROUBLE AT JAMESTOWN

Jamestown (1606–1616)

Cast of Characters (in order of appearance)

Albert: *Virginia Company man 1*

Thomas: *Virginia Company man 2*

Samuel: *Wealthy Jamestown settler*

Clancy: *Indentured servant*

John Smith: *English adventurer*

Powhatan: *Chief of 28 Native American tribes*

Nataquaus: *Powhatan's son*

Pocahontas: *Powhatan's daughter*

Opechancanough: *Powhatan's brother*

Powhatan's Men 1–4 (non-speaking roles)

Jamestown Settlers 1–4

John Rolfe: *Jamestown planter*

Lady-in-Waiting: *Queen's servant*

Queen Anne: *English queen*

10 Easy-to-Read American History Plays • Scholastic Professional Books © 2001

◄ ACT 1 ►

SCENE 1: THE VIRGINIA COMPANY OFFICE, APRIL 10, 1606

(Albert works at his desk. Thomas runs in.)

THOMAS: We got it! We got it!

ALBERT: Really? King James said yes?

THOMAS: Yes! The Virginia Company can send colonists to the New World!

ALBERT: Of course, the king will tell us what the settlers can and can't do.

THOMAS: Of course.

ALBERT: Of course, Virginia is a long way away. It's all the way on the other side of the Atlantic Ocean.

THOMAS: That's very true.

ALBERT: The colonists will have to make sure everyone obeys the rules.

THOMAS: Of course.

ALBERT: They'll also have to work hard. The Virginia Company is spending a lot of money to send people to the New World. We have to make money on the colony. The colonists have to understand that.

THOMAS: Hardworking, honest people—that's who we want.

SCENE 2: ON BOARD THE *SUSAN CONSTANT* IN THE MIDDLE OF THE ATLANTIC OCEAN, DECEMBER 1606

SAMUEL: You know it's really not fair, not fair at all. My oldest brother got all the land, the house, and most of the money. I can't help it if I wasn't born first. Hey! You! Clancy! Where's my tea?

CLANCY: Water's boiling, sir. *(muttering to himself)* I'll tell you what's not fair. I have to work for Sir Samuel for seven years. Then I'll finally be free. I can buy my own land. I won't have to work for anyone anymore.

SAMUEL: Make sure the water's hot, Clancy! Hot!

CLANCY *(muttering to himself)*: It's going to be a long seven years.

(Clancy leaves. John Smith enters.)

SAMUEL: Hey! You! Smith! John Smith!

JOHN SMITH: What can I do for you, Samuel?

SAMUEL: I've been thinking. I think I should be on the council. You need someone like me to tell everyone else what to do and how to do it.

JOHN SMITH: The Virginia Company's already decided who's going to be on the council. You know that. All the names are locked in a box. We'll open it when we land in Virginia.

SAMUEL: Well, I'm *sure* my name is in the box.

JOHN SMITH (*muttering to himself*): I'm sure hoping it's not.

SCENE 3: VIRGINIA, MAY 1607

POWHATAN: The English have maybe 100 men. They have three ships.

NATAQUAUS: They have three ships with cannons.

POWHATAN: We have 12,000 people to their 100 men. This is our home. We know where the game is. We know what grows well here. We know where to find water.

NATAQUAUS: The English think this is their home now. They say they want to be friends with us.

POWHATAN: I don't trust the English yet. Keep them busy. Make it hard for them to build their fort. Make it hard for them to plant their crops. Make it hard for them to live here.

NATAQUAUS: Yes, Father.

POCAHONTAS: Why did the English come here? Why did they leave their homes? England must be a very bad place to live.

POWHATAN: We will make them miss England.

━ ACT 2 ━

SCENE 1: THE BANKS OF THE CHICKAHOMINY RIVER, NEAR JAMESTOWN, DECEMBER 1607

CLANCY: Samuel is spitting mad that he's not on the council.

JOHN SMITH: I don't think he's ever worked hard a day in his life. That's the problem with too many of the settlers—and the indentured servants.

CLANCY: It's hard to work for something that's not yours.

JOHN SMITH: Everyone has to work hard now, or Jamestown won't make it. We won't survive.

CLANCY: So many of the men are sick. We left England with 140 colonists—half have died. There's not enough food. Winter's coming. The ships have gone back to England.

JOHN SMITH: Powhatan and his people are helping us now. They're giving us corn. They'll teach us how to live here. Shh! What's that noise? Who's there?

10 Easy-to-Read American History Plays • Scholastic Professional Books © 2001

(Nataquaus and Opechancanough jump in front of Clancy and Smith.)

OPECHANCANOUGH: John Smith. You're so far from Jamestown. Have you run away from your people?

JOHN SMITH: We're searching for food.

OPECHANCANOUGH: Don't worry, John Smith. We'll feed you. Take that one, Nataquaus. I'll take John Smith.

JOHN SMITH: Wait a minute!

(Opechancanough and Nataquaus lead John Smith and Clancy away.)

SCENE 2: POWHATAN'S CAMP, A MONTH LATER

POWHATAN: John Smith, I've enjoyed having you as a guest.

JOHN SMITH: I am not a guest. A guest can leave when he wishes. I'm a prisoner.

POWHATAN: I'm sorry you feel that way.

(Powhatan claps his hands. Opechancanough and Nataquaus make John Smith kneel down. A group of Powhatan's men surround Smith.)

JOHN SMITH: Wait a minute! What's going on?

(Pocahontas pushes through the men.)

POCAHONTAS: Stop!

SCENE 3: JAMESTOWN, A FEW DAYS LATER

JOHN SMITH: There are only 38 men still alive here at Jamestown! How can that be? I've been gone only a month!

SETTLER 1: Where were you exactly?

SETTLER 2: Smith told you. He was with Powhatan. *(turning to Smith)* What were you doing with Powhatan, Smith? We needed you here.

JOHN SMITH: Wait a minute! They captured me! They killed poor Clancy and—

SAMUEL: It's your fault, John Smith. It's all your fault that I've lost my servant. You should pay me for my loss.

SETTLER 3: And you say that Powhatan was about to kill you, but his daughter— his eleven-year-old daughter—saved your life? Hmm.

JOHN SMITH: We need to work together. Winter isn't over. We don't have time to sit around and talk.

10 Easy-to-Read American History Plays • Scholastic Professional Books © 2001

SETTLER 2: He's right. I'm hungry. I'm tired of being hungry. I'm cold. I'm tired of being cold.

SETTLER 1: Then go out and find some food. Go out and find some wood for a fire.

SETTLER 2: I've been sick. You go out.

SETTLER 1: I've been sick, too. Sicker than you.

SETTLER 2: Have not been sicker.

SETTLER 1: Have too been sicker.

JOHN SMITH: Wait a minute! That's enough!

SAMUEL: You owe me three thousand pounds, Smith. I'll give you six years to pay me.

SETTLER 3: You say Powhatan just let you go? Just like that? Hmm.

(Settler 4 comes running in.)

SETTLER 4: A ship! An English ship! We're saved!

(Everyone but Samuel runs out.)

SAMUEL *(calling after Smith)*: You! Smith! You'd better bring me some food from that ship! You owe me!

⮜ ACT 3 ⮞

SCENE 1: JAMESTOWN, 1609

SETTLER 1: "He who does not work, will not eat." If I hear Smith say that one more time, I'm going to eat my boots.

SETTLER 2: You ate your boots last month.

SETTLER 1: I shouldn't have to boil my boots and eat them. That's my point! John Smith isn't helping things. He's making them worse. We never should have elected him as president of the colony.

SETTLER 3: Powhatan attacks us all the time.

SETTLER 4: He gives us food sometimes.

SETTLER 3: Powhatan only sends Pocahontas here with food because he wants to know what's going on here in Jamestown.

SETTLER 1: John Smith's going back to England. I've written to the Virginia Company. They're going to call him back.

SAMUEL: He still owes me money.

10 Easy-to-Read American History Plays • Scholastic Professional Books © 2001

SCENE 2: JAMESTOWN, 1613

SETTLER 1: Hey, Pocahontas. I just got a letter from John Smith. It came all the way across the sea.

POCAHONTAS: How is he?

SETTLER 1: Why don't you come with me? I'll read it to you.

POCAHONTAS: Why don't you just tell me what John Smith said in his letter?

SETTLER 1: No, why don't you come with me?

POCAHONTAS: I don't think so.

SETTLER 1: I think so. *Grab her!*

(Settlers 2–4 rush out and grab Pocahontas.)

POCAHONTAS: Let me go!

SETTLER 3: No, you're going to stay here in Jamestown for a while.

SETTLER 2: We'll see what's more important to Powhatan—war with Jamestown or his daughter.

SETTLER 4: He won't attack us as long as Pocahontas is here.

SETTLER 1: Let's see if Powhatan will give us money for her.

POCAHONTAS: John Smith would never have done this!

SETTLER 3: That's why he got sent back to England.

SCENE 3: JAMESTOWN, 1614

JOHN ROLFE: Before you eat, you put a napkin in your lap.

POCAHONTAS: And I pick up the fork with my right hand?

JOHN ROLFE: Which hand do you use more—your right hand or your left hand?

POCAHONTAS: My right hand.

JOHN ROLFE: That's the hand you use then.

POCAHONTAS: Do you think the English can get along with my people?

JOHN ROLFE: We're at peace with your father now.

POCAHONTAS: Not many people here trust him—or me.

JOHN ROLFE: I do.

10 Easy-to-Read American History Plays • Scholastic Professional Books © 2001

POCAHONTAS: Tell me about England.

JOHN ROLFE: It's very far away. It rains a lot. Would you like to go there one day?

POCAHONTAS: I would go if I knew I could come back here.

JOHN ROLFE: You know, I've made some money raising tobacco. The English can't get enough of it. I was wondering . . .

POCAHONTAS: Wondering what?

JOHN ROLFE: Would you like to visit England with me? Would you marry me?

POCAHONTAS: I guess you think the English and my people *can* get along.

➤ ACT 4 ➤

WINDSOR CASTLE, ENGLAND, 1616

LADY-IN-WAITING: Here's another letter, your Majesty. It's from John Smith.

QUEEN ANNE: John Smith! Whatever does he want? Money for more adventures in the New World? Does he want me to send him back to Jamestown?

LADY-IN-WAITING: No ma'am. He says the Indian girl who saved his life is coming to England. She's married John Rolfe, the tobacco planter. John Smith thinks you should meet her.

QUEEN ANNE: It might be a good idea to meet her. It might make more people want to settle in Virginia. The more people who move there, the more land we can claim. He says this girl saved his life? What's her name?

LADY-IN-WAITING: It was Pocahontas, but now she's called Rebecca. Rebecca Rolfe.

QUEEN ANNE: I've never met an American before. It could be interesting.

10 Easy-to-Read American History Plays • Scholastic Professional Books © 2001

TEACHING GUIDE

Background

Founded on May 14, 1607, Jamestown, Virginia, was the first permanent English colony in America. The year before, King James I granted a charter to the Virginia Company that gave the company the right to settle, explore, and govern a portion of the so-called New World. The company hoped that its investment in the New World would bring large profits. Soon after, a group of about 100 men sailed out of London on the ships the *Godspeed,* the *Discovery,* and the *Susan Constant.*

The site of the new colony, named for King James I, was on a peninsula in the James River. The location was swampy and unhealthy; many of the men died of malaria or yellow fever during the first summer. That winter more colonists died of hunger despite the abundance of game and fish. The settlement was located in the midst of Powhatan's confederacy of 28 Native American tribes. The alliance was often uneasy; members fought with one another and harassed the colonists.

Captain John Smith emphasized that the colonists had to work together in order to survive, but many were more interested in searching for gold and silver and refused to help. On a scouting expedition for food, Smith was captured and taken to Powhatan. During some kind of ceremony, Pocahontas interceded on Smith's behalf; Smith believed that she had saved his life. About a month after his capture, Smith returned to Jamestown. He was elected president of the colony but proved unpopular with some of the colonists and was called back to London by the Virginia Company.

Pocahontas helped the colonists by bringing them food and warning Smith of imminent attacks by her father's tribes. In 1613 the Jamestown colonists kidnapped Pocahontas to use her as a negotiating tool with Powhatan. She became a Christian and married planter John Rolfe in 1614. Rolfe turned around Jamestown's fortunes by introducing a sweet tobacco; this "brown gold" became Virginia's cash crop. Tobacco is a labor-intensive crop, and in 1619 a Dutch ship brought the first enslaved Africans to America. In that same year, the first legislative assembly in America was held at Jamestown.

Vocabulary Some readers may not be familiar with the following words:

colonist: person who helps start or lives in a colony

colony: group of people who go to a different land but are still under the rule of the country from which they came

elected: chosen to serve in an office

indentured servant: person who must work for someone else for several years before earning freedom

settler: person who goes to live in a new country, colony, or region

Books to Build Interest

The Corn Raid: A Story of the Jamestown Settlement by James Lincoln Collier (NTC Publishing Group, 2000)

The Double Life of Pocahontas by Jean Fritz (Putnam Publishing Group, 1983)

John Smith by Charles Parlin Graves (Chelsea House, 1991)

A Lion to Guard Us by Clyde Robert Bulla (HarperCollins, 1989)

Web Sites

http://www.apva.org (Association for the Preservation of Virginia Antiquities)

http://ab.mec.edu/jamestown/glawp.html (Conant School, fourth grade)

10 Easy-to-Read American History Plays • Scholastic Professional Books © 2001

ACTIVITIES

Movie Magic?

Some of your students may have seen the animated movie *Pocahontas*. How historically accurate do they think the movie is? After students conduct more research into the events at Jamestown and learn more about John Smith, Pocahontas, and Powhatan, show the movie in class or have them watch it at home. In which instances was the movie accurate? How was it inaccurate? Pose questions such as the following: Why do they think the filmmakers altered the story? Do students feel that it's all right to alter the facts?

Rules for a New Colony

The Jamestown settlers were a long way from England. They still had to obey English laws and govern themselves. Ask students to draw up their own sets of rules for an imaginary American colony, on Mars for example, or another planet. What kind of government would they put in place? How would they ensure that all the colonists worked together? How would they deal with individuals who refused to work to help the colony? Discuss the various systems students devise, and then have the class work together to create one system of government and rules.

What Happened Before and After?

John Smith had many adventures in Jamestown, but even before that, he lived an exciting life. Once he was sold as a slave in Turkey, but there too, was rescued by a young woman. Pocahontas did travel to England with her husband John and son Thomas. She met King James and Queen Anne, but Pocahontas died in England. Powhatan lived a long life, but his people were displaced. Have students research these or other before-and-after stories.

Negotiating Peace

Powhatan was the leader of 28 different tribes. These tribes sometimes cooperated and sometimes fought among themselves, and with Jamestown. Divide the class into two groups, the English settlers at Jamestown and members of Powhatan's tribes. Challenge the two groups to negotiate a peace settlement with each other—and among themselves. Suggest that each group list what is necessary for its survival. How do the needs of the groups clash? How do they complement each other? How can the essential needs of both groups be met in a peaceful manner?

Jamestown Then and Now

Archaeologists are excavating the site of the original Jamestown settlement. To learn more about this project, students can visit the Association for the Preservation of Virginia Antiquities Web site referenced earlier. Encourage them to use this Web site as a springboard for Jamestown projects such as a diorama of the original Fort James or a travel brochure for Jamestown.

A Long Trip Across the Sea

Three ships left London, England, on December 20, 1606, for the New World. They arrived at the site of Jamestown on the James River in Virginia on May 13, 1607. Challenge students to trace the colonists' route across the Atlantic Ocean on a map. Then they can determine the total distance and find the average number of miles the ships traveled per day. Have students compare that rate of travel to present-day travel today on various means of transport.

10 Easy-to-Read American History Plays • Scholastic Professional Books © 2001

FISH HEADS AND SNAKE SKINS

The Pilgrims at Plymouth (1620-1621)

Cast of Characters (in order of appearance)

Joan Tilly: *Plymouth Pilgrim*

William Brewster: *One of the leaders of the Pilgrims*

John Tilly: *Plymouth Pilgrim*

Wrestling Brewster: *William and Mary Brewster's son*

Elizabeth Tilly: *Joan and John Tilly's daughter*

William Bradford: *Governor of Plymouth Colony*

Miles Standish: *English soldier*

Strangers 1–2 • Separatists 1–2

Rose Standish: *Miles Standish's wife*

Samoset: *Native American from the Abenaki tribe*

Squanto: *Native American man*

Narraganset Man

Massasoit: *Leader of the Wampanoag people*

Wampanoag People 1–4 (non-speaking roles)

10 Easy-to-Read American History Plays • Scholastic Professional Books © 2001

⮞ ACT 1 ⮜

SCENE 1: THE TILLY'S HOUSE IN LEIDEN, HOLLAND, 1618

JOAN TILLY: I don't want to move again. It was hard enough to leave England to come here. We can't go back to England. The king will have us put in jail. Where will we go?

WILLIAM BREWSTER: South America or Virginia.

JOHN TILLY: South America? It's too hot!

JOAN TILLY: And Virginia is so far away.

JOHN TILLY: Will they let us worship as we please?

WILLIAM BREWSTER: We could stay here in Holland. We don't have to leave.

JOHN TILLY: We've been here for twelve years, but none of us are making much money. Maybe it is time to move.

JOAN TILLY: Our daughter Elizabeth speaks Dutch all the time. She's forgotten she's English. At least Virginia is an English colony.

WILLIAM BREWSTER: We wouldn't have to live in Jamestown. We could start our own colony. Virginia covers hundreds of miles.

JOHN TILLY: Joan's right. It's an English colony. Will the king let us worship as we please in Virginia? Would we be safe there?

WILLIAM BREWSTER: We'll have to ask the Virginia Company and see what they say.

JOAN TILLY: It won't do any harm to ask.

SCENE 2: ON BOARD THE *MAYFLOWER* IN SOUTHAMPTON, ENGLAND, SEPTEMBER 16, 1620

WRESTLING BREWSTER: We're on our way! I can't believe we had to turn back two times!

ELIZABETH TILLY: I wish everyone had wanted to come to Virginia with us. I miss Anne. I'll never see her again. I'll never see my very best friend again.

WRESTLING BREWSTER: You'll make a new best friend.

ELIZABETH TILLY: We don't even know half the people on the *Mayflower*. Father calls them the Strangers. They call us Separatists.

WRESTLING BREWSTER: Not anymore! Now we are all called pilgrims.

ELIZABETH TILLY: I guess we'll get to know the Strangers soon enough. We're going to be living with them in Virginia.

10 Easy-to-Read American History Plays • Scholastic Professional Books © 2001

WRESTLING BREWSTER: Look! There's Miles Standish! He's already having the men drill with their weapons. I'm going to ask if I can drill with the men, too.

ELIZABETH TILLY: You're too young to be a soldier.

WRESTLING BREWSTER: You're just jealous because you're a girl.

ELIZABETH TILLY: I may be a girl, but I have enough work to do. I don't need to go out and be a soldier, too.

WRESTLING BREWSTER: You might. We're going to a whole new world. Who knows what kind of people live there? Or animals?

ELIZABETH TILLY: It's not like we'll be the first people who ever lived there. Lots of people are there already.

WRESTLING BREWSTER: Maybe Miles Standish will let me play the drum while the men march!

(Wrestling runs off.)

ELIZABETH TILLY: Maybe I will watch the men drill—just in case.

➤ ACT 2 ➤

ON BOARD THE *MAYFLOWER*, NOVEMBER 11, 1620

WILLIAM BRADFORD: The good news is that we have arrived. The bad news is that we have not arrived in Virginia. Our map says that this is Plymouth.

MILES STANDISH: The captain says it would be too dangerous to try to sail to Virginia. So it looks like we'll stay here. There's fresh water and a good harbor.

WILLIAM BRADFORD: We are not in Virginia. So the rules of the Virginia Company are no good here. We must draw up our own set of rules.

MILES STANDISH: There's been some trouble between the Strangers and the Separatists. It was a long and hard trip, but we're here now. We have to get along and work together.

WILLIAM BRADFORD: We've talked together and made up a set of rules for our Plymouth colony to follow. Each man will read them and then sign his name.

STRANGER 1: I paid my money to go to Virginia, not Plymouth! I'm not signing!

SEPARATIST 1: Unstop your ears! Didn't you hear Miles Standish? It's too dangerous! Do you know what the word *dangerous* means?

WILLIAM BRADFORD: Everybody calm down.

STRANGER 2 *(to Stranger 1)*: At least read the rules. You might even agree with them.

10 Easy-to-Read American History Plays • Scholastic Professional Books © 2001

STRANGER 1: I don't think so.

SEPARATIST 2: This may be even better than where we were going in Virginia.

STRANGER 1: I don't think so.

STRANGER 2: Just read the rules.

STRANGER 1: Don't tell me what to do.

SEPARATIST 1: Well, somebody's got to tell you what to do. You're nothing but a trouble-maker.

MILES STANDISH: That's enough. This is exactly why we need the Mayflower Compact. Nobody is a Stranger anymore. Nobody is a Separatist. We're one colony, working together, following the same rules.

STRANGER 1: All right, all right. Let me take a look at these rules of yours. Okay, it says that we make laws for the good of the colony. There's nothing wrong with that. Then it says that we make sure everybody follows the laws. There's nothing wrong with that.

WILLIAM BRADFORD: So you'll sign?

STRANGER 1: Of course I will. What makes you think I wouldn't?

SEPARATIST 1: I'll sign next.

STRANGER 2: Then I will.

WILLIAM BRADFORD: Then everyone will read and sign the compact?

(Everyone shouts: "Yes!")

⬩ ACT 3 ⬩

SCENE 1: A PLYMOUTH GARDEN, MARCH 16, 1621

ROSE STANDISH: It's been a terrible winter. We've had two fires.

JOAN TILLY: Luckily no one was hurt.

ROSE STANDISH: More than forty people have died since we got here.

JOAN TILLY: I wish the men could bury them during the day, and we could put stones on the graves.

ROSE STANDISH: We can't. We can't let the Indians know how many people we're losing. They might think they can attack us and wipe us out.

JOAN TILLY: I hope these seeds we're planting will grow.

ROSE STANDISH: It would be nice to have vegetables with the fish that the men catch.

(Samoset enters. Miles Standish and William Bradford go to meet him.)

JOAN TILLY: Oh my!

SAMOSET: Welcome, Englishmen!

MILES STANDISH: You speak English!

SAMOSET: English fishermen taught me. They come all the way here to fish for cod.

WILLIAM BRADFORD: My name is William Bradford. This is Miles Standish.

SAMOSET: My name is Samoset.

MILES STANDISH: I wish everyone were as friendly as you are.

SAMOSET: You have to understand. This used to be a Patuxet village. The English brought a sickness. Many people died. Then an English captain kidnapped some of our people. They don't trust you.

WILLIAM BRADFORD: Can you help us make friends with them? We don't want to hurt anyone.

SAMOSET: I can try. Good-bye, Englishmen.

SCENE 2: PLYMOUTH, SPRING OF 1621

WRESTLING BREWSTER: Dad! Samoset's coming back! He's got someone with him! Another Indian!

WILLIAM BREWSTER: Go tell Miles Standish. Quick!

(Samoset and Squanto enter. Brewster moves toward them slowly.)

WILLIAM BREWSTER: Hello! Good to see you again, Samoset! Who's this with you? A friend of yours?

SAMOSET: This is Squanto. His English is even better than mine. *(to Squanto)* Go on, say something.

SQUANTO: My manners are better, too.

WILLIAM BREWSTER *(laughing nervously)*: Oh, no! Samoset's been very polite. Oh, look! Here's Miles Standish! Look, Miles. Samoset's brought a friend.

MILES STANDISH: Just one friend, or are there more hiding in the woods?

SQUANTO: There's no need to hide in the woods. We come in peace.

SAMOSET: Squanto wants to stay and help you.

10 Easy-to-Read American History Plays • Scholastic Professional Books © 2001

SQUANTO: England is very different from this country. The plants are different. The weather is different. There are things you need to know.

WILLIAM BREWSTER: Your English is very good, Squanto. Where did you learn to speak it so well?

SAMOSET: He was kidnapped—taken away by an English captain. They sold him as a slave. He escaped. He's been to Spain and to England.

SQUANTO: Samoset loves to tell my story.

WILLIAM BREWSTER: Not all of my people are bad people.

SQUANTO: Not all of my people are bad, either.

MILES STANDISH: We could use some help.

SQUANTO: Good. Let's get started. What have you planted in your gardens?

SCENE 3: A FEW WEEKS LATER IN PLYMOUTH

SQUANTO: You see how the bean plants climb up the corn plants? If you plant beans and corn together, you save space.

ELIZABETH TILLY: And if you bury what's left of a fish in the ground by the plants, they'll grow tall and strong. That's what you said, right?

SQUANTO: Plants need to be fed, just like you and me.

(The Narraganset man enters. He carries a bunch of arrows with a rattlesnake skin around them.)

ELIZABETH TILLY: Who's that? Is he a friend of yours? What's he carrying?

SQUANTO: Please tell Governor Bradford to come here.

(Elizabeth leaves.)

SQUANTO: What do you want?

NARRAGANSET MAN: None of your business. Who's in charge here?

SQUANTO: Governor Bradford. He's coming.

(William Bradford comes in.)

WILLIAM BRADFORD: What's going on?

(The Narraganset man throws down the arrows at Bradford's feet.)

WILLIAM BRADFORD: What does that mean?

SQUANTO: It means the Narragansets want war. Shoot the snakeskin. Fill it with bullets.

10 Easy-to-Read American History Plays • Scholastic Professional Books © 2001

WILLIAM BRADFORD: Are you sure?

SQUANTO: Would you rather fight them?

(Bradford shoots the skin. The Narraganset looks at him with surprise.)

NARRAGANSET MAN (to Squanto): Is he crazy?

SQUANTO: No, he's just stronger than you are. Fight them and you will see.

NARRAGANSET MAN: Are you crazy? No way!

(He runs out.)

WILLIAM BRADFORD: What happened? Are we at war?

SQUANTO: No. Everything's fine.

ACT 4

PLYMOUTH, A FEW WEEKS LATER

WILLIAM BRADFORD: Oh, no! Now what?

(Squanto and Massasoit and the Wampanoag people enter.)

SQUANTO: Governor Bradford, this is Massasoit, the great chief I've been telling you about.

WILLIAM BRADFORD: Pleased to meet you, Massasoit.

MASSASOIT: We have some things to talk about. I wish to have peace between your people and mine.

WILLIAM BRADFORD: We want that, too.

MASSASOIT: I have come to say this: My people will not hurt any of your people. If we take your tools, they will be returned. If you take ours, they will be returned. If anyone makes war on us, you will help us.

WILLIAM BRADFORD: And if anyone makes war on us, you must help us. You must tell your friends and neighbors to leave us in peace.

MASSASOIT: We bring no weapons with us, you see. When you visit us, you must leave your weapons at home.

WILLIAM BRADFORD: We can do that.

(Bradford and Massasoit shake hands.)

WILLIAM BRADFORD: Here, my friend, let me show you around Plymouth.

10 Easy-to-Read American History Plays • Scholastic Professional Books © 2001

TEACHING GUIDE

Background

A small group of English Puritans known as the Separatists broke away from the Church of England. Some Separatists fled from the village of Scrooby to Amsterdam to avoid religious persecution. Dismayed that their children were growing up Dutch rather than English, and that they remained near the bottom of the economic ladder in Holland, about half of the Separatists decided to try their luck in the Virginia colony. Also sailing on board the *Mayflower* were other emigrants that the Separatists called "Strangers."

English merchant-adventurers underwrote the voyage; all the settlers agreed to work for seven years to pay them back. The *Mayflower* left England on September 16, 1620, with about 100 passengers. They sighted Cape Cod—not Virginia—on November 19, 1620. Because of bad weather and difficult sailing conditions, the Pilgrims decided to settle on Cape Cod. Their charter didn't cover this region, so the group wrote the Mayflower Compact, a set of rules and laws for the new colony.

On December 11, scouts found cleared fields and fresh water at Plymouth. Work on the new settlement began. Everyone remained on board the *Mayflower* that first winter while houses were built; over half the passengers and crew died of illness and malnutrition. Two fires endangered the new buildings at Plymouth. Samoset, an Abenaki Sagamore, appeared in the spring. He told the Pilgrims that a Patuxet village had occupied the site of Plymouth until it was wiped out by a plague. He also related that an English captain had kidnapped Native Americans from the region a few years earlier, and so they were leery of the English. Samoset returned later with Squanto (Tisquantum) who became the interpreter for the Pilgrims, Massasoit, and the Wampanoag people. The Pilgrims and the Wampanoag signed a peace treaty that would last over 50 years.

Vocabulary
Some readers may not be familiar with the following words:

drill: to teach by having a person do the same thing over and over

manners: polite ways of acting

weapon: object someone can use to attack or protect oneself

worship: to take part in a religious service

Books to Build Interest

A Journey to the New World: The Diary of Patience Whipple, Mayflower, 1620 by Kathryn Lasky (Scholastic, 1996)

N.C. Wyeth's Pilgrims by Robert San Souci (Chronicle, 1991)

Pilgrim Voices: Our First Year in the New World by Connie and Peter Roop (Walker, 1995)

The Pilgrims of Plimouth by Marcia Sewall (Atheneum, 1986)

Stranded at Plimoth Plantation, 1626 by Gary Bowen (HarperCollins, 1994)

Web Sites

http://www.plimoth.org (Web site of the Plimouth Plantation)

http://www.pilgrims.net (history of Plymouth, Massachusetts and its people)

10 Easy-to-Read American History Plays • Scholastic Professional Books © 2001

ACTIVITIES

Mapping Movement

Most of the Separatists moved from the village of Scrooby in Nottinghamshire, England, to Leiden in the Netherlands. Then they traveled to Southampton, England, where they eventually boarded the *Mayflower* for their journey to Plymouth. Have students create one map, or a series of maps, showing their travels. Make sure they include captions to describe the moves and the importance of each one.

The Mayflower

The *Mayflower* was a 180 tun—not ton—ship. A *tun* was a barrel, so the ship could carry 180 barrels. A little more than 100 passengers made the 65- or 66-day voyage. At one point, during heavy winds, a main beam cracked and the ship began to take on water. The *Mayflower* continued on its journey. One man was swept overboard, but he held onto a rope and was saved. Challenge students to find out more about the *Mayflower*. They can present their findings in a variety of ways: a fictional diary kept by one of the passengers, a drawing of the ship (including a cross-section), or a travel brochure.

What Would You Take?

It's one thing to move from one town to another, or from one house to another in the same town, but the Pilgrims moved to a new, relatively uninhabited country. They had to build their own shelter, hunt and fish, grow their own food, and make their own clothes and furniture. Ask students to consider what would be essential to take on such a journey. What personal items would they want to carry with them? What practical items would they take? Remind them to consider the limited amount of space on the *Mayflower*. Students can list what they would take and/or illustrate how they would pack it.

Compare Climates

As mentioned above, most of the Separatists came from Scrooby in England. Have pairs of students compare and contrast the climates of Scrooby and Plymouth. They can present their data in the form of a television weathercast, with each partner taking one of the locations and reporting on its weather. Students should do four weathercasts, one for each season. They can make weather maps with symbols to use as props.

Certificate of Thanks

What would the Pilgrims have done without the help of Squanto? Students can show their appreciation by making certificates of thanks. Each certificate should explain what Squanto did and how it helped the Plymouth colonists. Provide a variety of materials such as colored paper, markers, gold stars, and ribbon for students to use. Display the certificates on the wall.

The First Thanksgiving

There were many thanksgivings celebrated in America before the Pilgrims arrived. And in fact, Native American celebrations were harvest feasts rather than feasts of thanksgiving. Work with students in creating a timeline of thanksgiving celebrations in America; include those of Ponce de León, Rene de Laudonnière, Martin Frobisher, and Juan de Oñate. Explore the Web site for the Plimoth Plantation referenced on page 29 for more information.

10 Easy-to-Read American History Plays • Scholastic Professional Books © 2001

TEA OVERBOARD!

The Boston Tea Party (1773)

Cast of Characters (in order of appearance)

Mr. Green: *A tea agent for the East India Company*

John Hancock: *Boston merchant*

Mrs. Conrad: *Protestor against tea tax*

Protestors 1–4

Mrs. Mills: *Protestor against tea tax*

Mrs. Spencer: *Protestor against tea tax*

Captain Hardy: *British officer*

British Soldiers 1–4 (non-speaking roles)

Sam Adams: *Revolutionary leader*

Boston Women and Men 1–4 • Messenger (non-speaking role)

John Fulton: *Boston carpenter* • Sarah Fulton: *John's wife*

Colonists 1–5 • George Hewes: *Boston man*

Leonard Pitt: *Boston man* • British Captain

10 Easy-to-Read American History Plays • Scholastic Professional Books © 2001

ACT 1

SCENE 1: SHOP IN BOSTON, MASSACHUSETTS, JUNE 1773

MR. GREEN: John Hancock! Welcome to my shop. What can I get for you today? We just got some beautiful new things from England. And you know, I can sell you tea at a *much* lower price than anyone else.

JOHN HANCOCK: Yes, I heard that you'd been picked to sell tea for the East India Tea Company.

MR. GREEN: It's quite an honor, really!

JOHN HANCOCK: So you can sell tea at a lower price than Americans can.

MR. GREEN: Yes, isn't it wonderful? But I must tell you—I'm surprised that more people aren't coming in and buying tea.

JOHN HANCOCK: Maybe they don't like King George telling them whom they can buy tea from and whom they can't.

MR. GREEN: That's not true! They can buy tea from anyone they want to. It's just that the East India Tea Company can sell its tea for the very lowest price.

JOHN HANCOCK: Then there's the tax on tea. Some people might have problems with that.

MR. GREEN: Some people might not like to buy tea that's been smuggled in. That's where all the American merchants get their tea. Smuggling is against the law.

JOHN HANCOCK: The colonies are British, but we have no voice in the British government. We have no say over taxes, or how they are spent.

MR. GREEN: That's not my fault!

JOHN HANCOCK: You could stop selling tea from the East India Tea Company.

MR. GREEN: You could stop causing trouble for merchants like me!

JOHN HANCOCK: I couldn't do that. But I could stop buying anything from merchants like you. Good day, sir.

SCENE 2: OUTSIDE THE MEETING HOUSE IN PEPPERELL, MASSACHUSETTS, A FEW WEEKS LATER

MRS. CONRAD: Ladies, we are here today to speak out against the tea tax!

PROTESTOR 1: Down with King George!

PROTESTOR 2: No more taxes!

PROTESTOR 3: We need to do more than speak out! We need to do something!

PROTESTOR 4: Burn the tea!

10 Easy-to-Read American History Plays • Scholastic Professional Books © 2001

MRS. MILLS: Did everyone bring their British tea?

PROTESTORS 1–4: *Yes!*

MRS. SPENCER: Dump it on the steps of the meeting house! Show King George how we feel about his taxes!

(As the protestors pour their tea, the British captain and soldiers come in. The women set the tea on fire.)

CAPTAIN HARDY: Ladies, ladies! What's going on here? What's all the noise about?

MRS. CONRAD: We don't want your British tea!

CAPTAIN HARDY: Here now, that's perfectly good tea! What are you doing? Put out that fire, I say! Put it out at once!

MRS. MILLS: Stand back, Captain.

MRS. SPENCER: We did buy this tea, Captain. We paid the tax on it. It is our tea. We can do what we want with it.

MRS. CONRAD: It's not against the law to burn tea, Captain.

MRS. MILLS: Not yet anyway.

PROTESTOR 1: Go back to England, you redcoats!

CAPTAIN HARDY *(muttering to himself)*: I wish I were back in England. *(to soldiers)* Leave the women alone. Let them burn their tea. Just make sure their fire doesn't spread.

PROTESTOR 2: It's too late. This fire is spreading all over the colonies.

CAPTAIN HARDY: Don't you worry, King George will put out your fire.

PROTESTOR 3: Let him try.

➤ ACT 2 ➤

SCENE 1: OLD SOUTH CHURCH IN BOSTON, DECEMBER 16, 1773

SAM ADAMS: Three ships loaded with English tea sit in our harbor. We have said that we don't want this tea. We have said that these ships should—must—sail back to England.

BOSTON WOMAN 1: With their tea!

SAM ADAMS: With their tea. Governor Hutchinson says the ships will stay here. We say to him—again—that the ships must leave our harbor. We say, also, that the British warships in the harbor must also leave.

BOSTON MAN 1: We don't want their tea!

BOSTON WOMAN 2: We don't want their taxes!

10 Easy-to-Read American History Plays • Scholastic Professional Books © 2001

BOSTON MAN 2: We don't want British soldiers in our homes!

(The messenger comes in and whispers in Sam Adams's ear.)

SAM ADAMS: Governor Hutchinson has left town. We have our answer.

BOSTON WOMAN 1: Do we want their tea?

BOSTON MAN 1: *No!* To the harbor!

BOSTON WOMAN 2: Throw the tea into the harbor!

BOSTON MAN 2: Let Governor Hutchinson and the British try to fish the tea out of the harbor!

SCENE 2: SARAH AND JOHN FULTON'S HOUSE IN BOSTON, LATER THAT NIGHT

JOHN FULTON: Now, remember, nobody takes any tea. We dump all of it overboard.

SARAH FULTON: Here, we'll rub coal dust on your face and hands. Wrap yourselves in these blankets.

COLONIST 1: Do you think the British know what we're up to?

COLONIST 2: Not a chance.

COLONIST 3: Governor Hutchinson left town, didn't he? If he thought there'd be trouble, he wouldn't have left.

COLONIST 4: We'll need axes to break open the chests.

JOHN FULTON: Remember this—do no harm to the ships or their crews.

GEORGE HEWES: What about the warships? What if they start firing on us?

JOHN FULTON: It's dark tonight. We'll have to get to the ships quickly. They won't fire on their own ships.

SARAH FULTON: Come over here, John Fulton. You need more coal dust on your face. *(whispering to him)* You'd better come back to me safe and sound.

JOHN FULTON: Don't worry. The British won't know what hit them.

SARAH FULTON: We'll follow you down to the harbor.

⟶ ACT 3 ⟵

SCENE 1: ON BOARD THE *DARTMOUTH* IN BOSTON HARBOR, LATER THAT NIGHT

LEONARD PITT: George Hewes, find the captain and bring him here. Make sure he has the keys. Get some candles from him, too.

(George Hewes leaves.)

LEONARD PITT: The rest of you get to work on the chests of tea.

(Colonists 1–5 open the chests and throw the tea overboard. George Hewes and the captain come in.)

LEONARD PITT: Good evening, Captain. May I have your keys?

CAPTAIN: You may. I only ask this of you—do not hurt my ship or my men.

LEONARD PITT: You have my word. Our fight is not with you or your men.

(The colonists work quickly and quietly. After throwing the tea overboard, they sweep and clean the decks. Colonist 5 slips some tea into his pocket.)

GEORGE HEWES: Hold on! What did you just put in your pocket?

COLONIST 5: Nothing.

GEORGE HEWES: We said we'd take no tea.

COLONIST 5: We've dumped almost 400 chests of tea into the harbor. Nobody's going to miss this little bit of tea.

LEONARD PITT: We are not thieves. Empty your pockets. Good. Now, throw him overboard. Let him swim back.

(The colonists take Colonist 5 and throw him into the water.)

LEONARD PITT: Here are your keys, Captain. I think you'll find your ship is in good condition.

CAPTAIN: I hope you know what you have started.

LEONARD PITT: We did not start it. King George did. But we will end it. Good night, Captain.

SCENE 2: THE FULTONS' HOUSE, LATER THAT NIGHT

SARAH FULTON: Thank goodness, the British warships didn't fire on you. You're sure no one was hurt?

JOHN FULTON: A couple of men had to swim back. Wasn't that something to see—all that tea floating in the harbor?

SARAH FULTON: I've never heard Boston so quiet.

JOHN FULTON: It won't be quiet for long.

SARAH FULTON: No, King George and Governor Hutchinson will have a lot to say when they hear about Boston's little tea party.

TEACHING GUIDE

Background

As a result of winning the French and Indian War, England gained the territory between the Appalachian Mountains and the Mississippi River. England had to protect that area as well as the 13 colonies, and the war had vastly increased its debt. The British Parliament decided to tax the colonists to pay for armies and forts in the new territory and to pay down England's war debt.

In 1764 the Sugar Act went into effect. Colonists had to pay import duties on molasses, sugar, wine and other goods. To stop the smuggling of these items, revenue officers wanted to be able to search homes. To further increase revenue, the Stamp Act was implemented in 1765. Colonial newspapers, and legal and business documents were taxed. Another act, the Quartering Act, said that the colonies would have to pay some of the costs of the British soldiers stationed there.

Each colony had a legislative assembly, and the assemblies voiced their outrage at these acts. A boycott on taxed goods began. Since they weren't represented in Parliament, the colonies insisted that the taxes were a form of taxation without representation. The Stamp Act was overturned by Parliament, but it reiterated that it had the right to tax the colonies.

In 1767 the Townshend Act taxed lead, paint, glass, paper, and tea imported to the colonies. That money would be used by Parliament to pay for British officials posted in America. The colonies protested. If they weren't able to show their disapproval of a British official by stopping his salary, then colonial self-government would be at risk. Most of the Townshend Act was repealed, except for the tax on tea. The colonies seemed to accept that tax, although much of the tea entering the colonies was smuggled in. Trouble broke out in 1773 when the East India Company was allowed to sell its tea more cheaply in the colonies than local merchants could sell theirs. The cities of Philadelphia and New York refused to let the East India Company's ships unload their tea. Boston held its famous tea party.

In response, Parliament passed the Intolerable Acts in 1774. The port of Boston was to be closed until the East India Company was paid for its losses, self-government in Massachusetts was limited, British officials accused of crimes in the colonies were to be tried in England, and British soldiers could be housed in Boston taverns and other empty buildings. Thanks to the Intolerable Acts, the 13 colonies banded together for the first time.

Vocabulary Some readers may not be familiar with the following words:

condition: the way a thing is

smuggle: to bring into a country in a way that is against the law

tax: money that people pay to their government

Books to Build Interest

The Boston Tea Party by Steven Kroll (Holiday House, 1998)

Emma's Journal by Marissa Moss (Harcourt Brace and Co., 1999)

The Liberty Tree: The Beginning of the American Revolution by Lucille Recht (Random House, 1998)

Sam Adams by Dennis Fradin (Houghton Mifflin, 1998)

Web Site

http://www.historyplace.com/united states/revolution/index.html (History Place)

10 Easy-to-Read American History Plays • Scholastic Professional Books © 2001

ACTIVITIES

Express Yourself

People often use bumper stickers and buttons—even slogans on T-shirts—to express their opinions. Ask students to think of slogans the colonists might have used to show their support for or opposition to the tax on tea, and opinions on the Boston Tea Party itself. Encourage them to illustrate their slogans, too. Post students' slogans on a bulletin board.

King George's View of the Boston Tea Party

Pose the following question for class discussion or writing prompts: What would you do if you were King George, and you found out about the Boston Tea Party? Then have students research how the king really reacted. Discuss whether they agree or disagree with his actions.

Beverage Boycott

To protest the tea tax, many colonists stopped drinking tea. Explain to students that when people *boycott* a product, they stop buying it, usually in protest. Survey students to find out what their favorite beverage is. What, if anything, would prompt them to boycott that beverage? Extend the activity to include other things such as clothing, movies, a specific business, and so on.

Spotlight on the Boston Tea Party

Magazines like *Cobblestone* often focus on a specific historical event. The entire issue is devoted to different articles about that event. Web pages, too, often highlight certain historical events. Let students work in groups to prepare their own magazine or Web page based on the Boston Tea Party. Emphasize that they should use a variety of ways to present their information—facts, biographies of the people involved, maps, timelines, illustrations, stories, poems, and quotes.

A Big Bill

The colonists in Boston destroyed tea worth about £15,000. (Today £1 is worth about $1.60.) The tea belonged to the East India Tea Company, but who should pay the company for its loss? Have students decide who should pay and then prepare a bill for the tea, including an explanation of why that person or those persons are responsible for the debt.

New Money

In 1765, the British passed the Currency Act. It prohibited colonists from printing and issuing their own money. This move helped unite the colonies. Assign students the task of designing paper money and coins for the 13 colonies. After the class has seen and studied all the designs, vote on which currency to use. Encourage students to compromise and include elements from different designs.

THE BRITISH ARE COMING!

Paul Revere's Ride (1775)

Cast of Characters (in order of appearance)

Jane Harrison: *Sarah Revere's friend*

Sarah Revere: *Paul Revere's daughter*

Rachel Revere: *Paul Revere's wife*

Paul Revere: *Boston silversmith*

Dr. Joseph Warren: *Patriot and a friend of Paul Revere*

John Larkin: *Patriot sympathizer*

American Sentry

Sam Adams • John Hancock

William Dawes • Dr. Samuel Prescott

British Soldiers 1–5

10 Easy-to-Read American History Plays • Scholastic Professional Books © 2001

⬩ ACT 1 ⬩

THE REVERE HOUSE IN BOSTON, APRIL 1, 1775

JANE HARRISON: I know what your father does.

SARAH REVERE: Everybody in Boston knows what he does. He's a silversmith. He makes beautiful things out of silver.

JANE HARRISON: He's a spy.

SARAH REVERE: What!?

JANE HARRISON: He spies on the British soldiers and then he tells Sam Adams and the Sons of Liberty what the soldiers are doing.

SARAH REVERE: Sam Adams is my father's friend. They talk about all kinds of things.

JANE HARRISON: My father says your father rode to New York and Philadelphia to tell everybody about the Boston Tea Party.

SARAH REVERE: The Boston Tea Party wasn't a secret. He could tell anybody about it if he wanted to.

JANE HARRISON: My father says your father rides around the colonies and spreads trouble. My father's a Loyalist. He's loyal to King George and to England. He says men like Sam Adams and John Hancock and your father are wrong to talk against the king.

SARAH REVERE: My father says a king should understand who and what he rules. King George has never visited America. He doesn't understand our problems here.

JANE HARRISON: So you think it's okay if your father talks against the king and England?

SARAH REVERE: He's not talking against the king. He wants the king to listen to what the colonists have to say.

JANE HARRISON: My father says men like your father are going to get us all in trouble . . . maybe we shouldn't be friends anymore.

SARAH REVERE: Maybe we shouldn't.

⬩ ACT 2 ⬩

SCENE 1: THE REVERE HOUSE, APRIL 18, 1775

RACHEL REVERE: Sarah and Jane Harrison still aren't speaking to each other.

PAUL REVERE: Jane's father still hasn't gotten over the tea party. He lost almost 50 chests of tea. That was a lot of money.

RACHEL REVERE: I've told all the children that they may lose more friends. I haven't told them that we may be at war with England soon. Maybe it won't come to that.

PAUL REVERE: I hope it doesn't, but we've got plenty of guns and powder stored in Concord—just in case.

RACHEL REVERE: Do you think Sam and John are safe in Lexington? If the British find them, will they really be sent to England to stand trial?

PAUL REVERE: King George wants to show everybody he's in charge here.

RACHEL REVERE: I've started buying extra food and knitting more socks for everybody—

(There is a knock on the door. Dr. Joseph Warren enters.)

DR. JOSEPH WARREN: Sorry to bother you, but it's important.

RACHEL REVERE: Come in. Would you like some coffee?

DR. JOSEPH WARREN: No time. The British are about to march to Lexington to grab Sam and John. We think they've found out about the weapons in Concord, too. We need you to ride to Lexington and Concord and warn everybody.

PAUL REVERE: Are the British marching out Boston Neck, or are they going to row across the Charles River?

DR. JOSEPH WARREN: We don't know yet.

PAUL REVERE: If it's by Boston Neck, hang one lantern in Christ Church tower. If it's by the river, hang two lanterns.

RACHEL REVERE: Be careful, Paul. The British know who you are.

⬿ ACT 3 ⬿

SCENE 1: ACROSS THE CHARLES RIVER IN CHARLESTOWN, A FEW HOURS LATER

JOHN LARKIN: There are two lanterns hanging in the tower, Paul. The British are rowing across the Charles River. They won't be too far behind you.

PAUL REVERE: I hope this is a fast horse.

JOHN LARKIN: It's the only horse I've got, but he's fast enough. Good luck to you.

(Revere hops on the horse and rides away.)

JOHN LARKIN (shouting after Revere): Bring my horse back, if you can!

(Revere rides through the countryside.)

PAUL REVERE: The British are coming! The British are coming! Get ready!

10 Easy-to-Read American History Plays • Scholastic Professional Books © 2001

SCENE 2: NEAR LEXINGTON, A FEW MINUTES LATER

PAUL REVERE: Arm yourselves! The British are coming!

AMERICAN SENTRY: Stop making all that noise!

PAUL REVERE: Noise! You'll have more noise than this before long. The British are coming!

AMERICAN SENTRY: Well, why didn't you say so? *(shouting)* The British are coming! Arm yourselves! The British are coming!

(Sam Adams and John Hancock rush out.)

SAM ADAMS: So they're coming at last?

PAUL REVERE: Yes, and they're coming for you and John. You've got to get out of here—fast!

JOHN HANCOCK: Don't worry—we're ready to go. What about you? The British will be after you, too.

(William Dawes comes riding in.)

WILLIAM DAWES: The British are coming!

REVERE, ADAMS, HANCOCK *(all together)*: We know, Dawes.

WILLIAM DAWES: Well, don't just stand there. Get a move on!

(The four men shake hands. Sam and John leave.)

WILLIAM DAWES: I came a different way, in case you didn't make it. I'm glad to see you did.

PAUL REVERE: The British know about the guns at Concord. Somebody's got to warn the Americans there.

WILLIAM DAWES: Let's go then!

(Revere and Dawes ride off. They are soon joined by Dr. Samuel Prescott on horseback.)

DR. SAMUEL PRESCOTT: The British are everywhere! They know that John and Sam left Lexington!

WILLIAM DAWES: We've still got a head start. We'll make it to Concord.

PAUL REVERE: If we run into the British, we should try to split up. That way, at least one of us should be able to make it to Concord.

(Four British soldiers step out and surround Revere, Dawes, and Prescott.)

BRITISH SOLDIER 1: And just where do you think you're going?

10 Easy-to-Read American History Plays • Scholastic Professional Books © 2001

BRITISH SOLDIER 2: Hey!

(Dr. Prescott manages to ride away.)

PAUL REVERE: He's a doctor. Someone had a bad accident. We rode to get him.

WILLIAM DAWES *(shouting at the top of his lungs):* The Americans are coming!

BRITISH SOLDIER 3: Where! Where are they!

(The British soldiers look around in surprise. William Dawes rides away.)

BRITISH SOLDIER 4: It's a trick! Hang on to that one!

BRITISH SOLDIER 1: He's not going anywhere—not on this horse anyway. I need a new horse. And it looks like I got one.

BRITISH SOLDIER 2: Take him back to Lexington. Let's find out what he knows.

SCENE 3: LEXINGTON, A FEW MINUTES LATER

BRITISH SOLDIER 3: You know who this is? It's Paul Revere, that's who.

BRITISH SOLDIER 4: It's a little late to be delivering a silver teapot, isn't it, Revere?

PAUL REVERE: I couldn't sleep. I thought I'd take a little ride.

BRITISH SOLDIER 1: You thought you'd take a little ride to warn your pals, Sam Adams and John Hancock, that we're after them.

PAUL REVERE: I heard they were in Philadelphia.

BRITISH SOLDIER 2: Philadelphia! That's a good one! You were just here in Lexington to warn them.

BRITISH SOLDIER 3: We know you're an express rider for the Massachusetts colony. We know you carry messages to New York and Philadelphia.

PAUL REVERE: I like to travel.

BRITISH SOLDIER 4: You like to travel, do you? How'd you like to travel to England to stand trial for treason?

PAUL REVERE: I haven't done anything wrong.

(Another British soldier runs in.)

BRITISH SOLDIER 5: What are you doing? Get to Concord—*now!* The Americans are attacking us!

(The British soldiers run out and leave Revere behind.)

PAUL REVERE: So it's started. The fight has started.

10 Easy-to-Read American History Plays • Scholastic Professional Books © 2001

TEACHING GUIDE

Background

By 1775 the population of the American colonies was about two million. But despite their wealth of resources, Americans still had to rely on British manufacturers, shipowners, and merchants. Many resources were shipped to England, turned into goods, some of which were shipped back to be sold to the colonists. England continued to see the colonies as a possession to be exploited. The colonists began to see freedom from England as the only way to bring manufacturing to America, and to keep the wealth at home.

The colonists began to organize themselves. They started "committees of correspondence" where local people acted together and established contact with colonists in more remote regions. These committees of correspondence evolved into effective local governments when the war broke out. At a higher level, provincial congresses met. Many of their members belonged to colonial assemblies. Their meetings were outlawed by the British governors. During the war, these bodies made laws and raised money and troops. The Continental Congress, the highest body, met in Philadelphia in 1774. It railed against taxation without representation and the Intolerable Acts. The British Parliament was itself divided on what to do about America.

On March 5, 1770, British soldiers fired into a crowd of Boston citizens. Five men were killed in the Boston Massacre, and several were wounded. That, and the enforcement of the Intolerable Acts, angered many colonists. On the night of April 18, 1775, word came that the British were marching to Lexington to arrest Sam Adams and John Hancock. They would send the men to England to stand trial. The British would then march on to Concord where colonists had stockpiled guns and ammunition. Paul Revere, William Dawes, and Dr. Samuel Prescott started out separately to warn Lexington and Concord and met one another on the road to Lexington. The Americans and British fought at Lexington and Concord, the first battles of the American Revolution.

Vocabulary Some readers may not be familiar with the following words:

delivering: taking something and leaving it at the right place

lantern: light inside a case of glass

loyal: faithful

sentry: guard, usually a soldier

treason: the act of being unfaithful to one's country

Books to Build Interest

Daughter of Liberty by Robert Quackenbush (Hyperion, 1998)

If You Lived at the Time of the American Revolution by Kay Moore (Scholastic, 1998)

A Picture Book of Paul Revere by David A. Adler (Holiday House, 1995)

Web Sites

http://www.netten.net/~bmassey/paulrevere.html (Longfellow's poem)

http://www.paulreverehouse.org (web site by the Paul Revere Memorial Association)

ACTIVITIES

Spread the Word

Paul Revere was an express rider who passed news and information from Boston to the other colonies, especially the cities of New York and Philadelphia. He spread the word about the Boston Tea Party, and on December 1774, he rode through treacherous weather to Portsmouth, New Hampshire, to warn of a British landing. Remind students that express riders were the fastest means of communication then. How would students quickly spread the word about an important event? To emphasize how communication has changed since 1775, work with the class to create a timeline showing advances in communication. Have them include other important events in American history on the timeline.

From the Horse's Point of View

Evidence suggests that Joseph Larkin's horse, Brown Beauty, was not returned. Students can stretch their imaginations by thinking about the ride from the horse's point of view. Encourage them to write the horse's account, including what happened before and after the ride, and to illustrate their work.

The Shot Heard 'Round the World

The fighting at Lexington and Concord marked the beginning of the American Revolution. Paul Revere was released in time to see the fighting break out in Lexington. The battles of Breed's Hill and Bunker Hill soon occurred in Boston. Let groups of students research these battles. They may present their findings in a variety of ways such as a play, the diary of a soldier or Boston citizen, or enactments of the battles using toy soldiers in a diorama.

Paul Revere's Ride

Paul Revere had to know whether the British were marching by land or by sea so he wouldn't get cut off. Students can add a map of Paul Revere's route (and William Dawes's and Dr. Samuel Prescott's routes) to their map books. Ask students: If you were the British, would you have taken a water or land route? Why?

"The Midnight Ride of Paul Revere"—Fact or Fiction?

In 1860, Henry Wadsworth Longfellow wrote the poem "The Midnight Ride of Paul Revere" and made Revere famous. How factual is the poem? Have students conduct research about the famous midnight ride and compare the facts to the poem. Suggest that they write their own poem or song about Paul Revere and his ride.

Becoming an Apprentice

Paul Revere trained apprentices in his shop to become silversmiths like he was. Apprentices learn a craft or trade from someone who has been in that field for a long time. What craft or trade would students like to learn? Who would they want to teach them? Let students write a letter to that person asking to be an apprentice. Remind them to list their skills and why they think they would be good apprentices.

10 Easy-to-Read American History Plays • Scholastic Professional Books © 2001

MOLLY PITCHER
Valley Forge (1777–1778)

Cast of Characters (in order of appearance)

Molly Dillon: *Twelve-year-old girl*

Jake Dillon: *Molly's older brother*

Eva Dillon: *Molly and Jake's grandmother*

Lyle Dillon: *Molly and Jake's grandfather*

George Washington: *Commander of the Continental army*

Martha Washington: *George Washington's wife*

Mary (Molly) Hays: *Woman known as Molly Pitcher*

William Hays: *Mary Hays's husband, a gunner in the Pennsylvania Artillery*

Baron von Steuben: *German military man*

Joseph Martin: *Private in the Continental Army*

American Soldiers 1–4

10 Easy-to-Read American History Plays • Scholastic Professional Books © 2001

ACT 1

SCENE 1: VALLEY FORGE, PENNSYLVANIA, IN THE PRESENT

MOLLY DILLON: I always thought there was a big fight at Valley Forge.

JAKE DILLON: No, this is where George Washington and his soldiers camped out.

EVA DILLON: It's a good thing there wasn't any fighting. A lot of the soldiers didn't even have shoes to wear. They had to wrap cloth around their feet.

LYLE DILLON: Washington was keeping his eye on Howe. Howe was the British general who had captured Philadelphia. Philadelphia was the American capital then. Howe made himself at home and waited until the winter was over to fight again.

MOLLY DILLON: Then why didn't Washington just march in and take Philadelphia back?

JAKE DILLON: He didn't have enough food and supplies for his soldiers. There weren't many factories in America then. The colonists used to buy most things from England.

EVA DILLON: The American soldiers weren't very good fighters, either. They were mostly farmers.

LYLE DILLON: Luckily, Baron von Steuben from Germany and Lafayette from France helped train the soldiers at Valley Forge.

EVA DILLON: Martha Washington was there, that winter, and so was a woman named Mary Ludwig Hays.

MOLLY DILLON: Mary Ludwig Hays? I've never heard of her.

JAKE DILLON: You were named after her.

MOLLY DILLON: Molly Pitcher? Molly Pitcher was at Valley Forge?

SCENE 2: GEORGE WASHINGTON'S HEADQUARTERS AT VALLEY FORGE, PENNSYLVANIA, WINTER OF 1777

GEORGE WASHINGTON: I have over 10,000 men here. I need at least 35,000 pounds of meat and 200 pounds of flour every day to feed them. I don't have the money to buy the food. And even if I did, we don't have the wagons to bring supplies here.

MARTHA WASHINGTON: So many of the men are sick, George. A lot of them are leaving, too. They're going back home.

GEORGE WASHINGTON: They're not soldiers yet. They're still farmers and merchants. If we're going to win this war—and our freedom—I have to turn them into soldiers.

MARTHA WASHINGTON: They're worried about their families and their farms and stores. I know how hard it is to run a farm while your husband's away. I'll be back at Mount Vernon in a few months when it's time to plant. You'll be here.

10 Easy-to-Read American History Plays • Scholastic Professional Books © 2001

(There is a knock at the door.)

GEORGE WASHINGTON: Come in!

(Mary and William Hays enter.)

MARY HAYS: Good afternoon, Colonel Washington, Mrs. Washington. This is my husband William. He's come to cut your hair, sir.

GEORGE WASHINGTON: Molly says you're a barber, William.

WILLIAM HAYS: Yes, sir, back in Pennsylvania I was—before the war.

MARY HAYS: I brought your laundry, ma'am.

MARTHA WASHINGTON: Thank you, Molly.

(William starts to cut Washington's hair. Mrs. Washington and Molly fold the clothes.)

GEORGE WASHINGTON: How's your hut, William? Are you warm enough?

WILLIAM HAYS: Yes, sir. I've got shoes, too. I'm luckier than some.

GEORGE WASHINGTON: You're with the artillery?

WILLIAM HAYS: Yes, sir.

GEORGE WASHINGTON: We're going to need you in the spring. With the help of your guns, I'm going to chase General Howe all the way back to England.

WILLIAM HAYS: Yes, sir. How much should I cut, sir?

SCENE 3: VALLEY FORGE, PENNSYLVANIA, MAY 5, 1778

BARON VON STEUBEN: Forward, march! Straight lines! Eyes in front of you! Guns held tight! Don't step on each other! Good! Good! Fall out! Take a five-minute break!

WILLIAM HAYS: My feet are about to fall off.

JOSEPH MARTIN: It feels like mine fell off two miles ago.

SOLDIER 1: We're better soldiers for all the marching.

SOLDIER 2: It's true. We need the practice. We wouldn't be here if we hadn't messed up in Germantown.

SOLDIER 3: I was there. Believe me, it's no fun to be fired at by your own soldiers. I'm lucky one of you sharpshooters didn't get me.

SOLDIER 4: It was the fog. You couldn't see two inches in front of your face—

SOLDIER 1: That was a sorry day—two American units shooting at each other.

SOLDIER 2: It was an accident—

10 Easy-to-Read American History Plays • Scholastic Professional Books © 2001

WILLIAM HAYS: We can't let accidents like that happen again.

JOSEPH MARTIN: If it happens once, it's an accident. If it happens again, we deserve to get beat by the British.

BARON VON STEUBEN: Everybody fall in! Forward, march! Good! Straight lines! Stand tall! Good!

(George Washington comes in. He goes to Von Steuben.)

GEORGE WASHINGTON: They're looking more and more like soldiers, Baron.

BARON VON STEUBEN: The British will think so, too. What can I do for you, General?

GEORGE WASHINGTON: Good news. France recognizes us as an independent country. They're going to help us against the British.

BARON VON STEUBEN: I don't think King George will like that.

⬩ ACT 2 ⬩

SCENE 1: MONMOUTH, NEW JERSEY, IN THE PRESENT

LYLE DILLON: The French said they were going to help America in the war. The English didn't like that. They were afraid France would send ships and cut off supplies to their troops in Philadelphia.

EVA DILLON: General Clinton had taken over for General Howe. King George told General Clinton to move his soldiers from Philadelphia to New York City.

JAKE DILLON: George Washington followed General Clinton. The American soldiers really had turned into soldiers by then. The Americans and the British fought right here in Monmouth.

MOLLY DILLON: Don't forget Molly Pitcher. Hey! If her real name was Mary Hays, how come she's called Molly Pitcher?

EVA DILLON: That happened right here, at the Battle of Monmouth.

SCENE 2: MONMOUTH, NEW JERSEY, JUNE 28, 1778

SOLDIER 1: It must be a hundred degrees out here. I sure could use some water.

SOLDIER 2: Don't think about how thirsty you are. Think about making things hotter for the British. Ow! I've been hit!

(Soldier 2 falls to the ground.)

SOLDIER 3: Watch out! There's someone over there by the trees!

SOLDIER 4: Hold it! It's a woman! What's that she's carrying? A pitcher?

10 Easy-to-Read American History Plays • Scholastic Professional Books © 2001

SOLDIER 3: Lady! There's a war going on here!

MARY HAYS (to Soldier 2): Let me take a look at your leg. It's not too bad. There, it's stopped bleeding. You'll be fine.

SOLDIER 1: Is that water in that pitcher?

MARY HAYS: It sure is. You can't fight a war if you're thirsty. Fill your canteens.

SOLDIER 4: I thought I was dreaming when I saw you with that pitcher of water.

SOLDIER 3: What's your name?

MARY HAYS: Mary Hays, but most people call me Molly. Here you are—full canteens. Good luck, boys.

(Mary leaves.)

SOLDIER 2: Hey! Thanks, Molly! Thanks, Molly Pitcher!

SCENE 3: MONMOUTH, NEW JERSEY, LATER THAT DAY

WILLIAM HAYS: I need more powder in the gun, Joseph.

JOSEPH MARTIN: Do you think we're winning or losing, Will? Those British guns never seem to stop!

WILLIAM HAYS: Winning, of course.

MARY HAYS: Our men are looking strong.

WILLIAM HAYS: I worry about you going around, giving them water, and taking care of them. Why don't you stay here for a while? I don't feel—

JOSEPH MARTIN: Look out!

(William Hays falls to the ground.)

MARY HAYS: Will!

WILLIAM HAYS: I'm all right. Just let me lie here for a while.

MARY HAYS: Are you sure you're all right?

WILLIAM HAYS: It's the heat, that's all.

JOSEPH MARTIN: We need somebody over here to work the guns!

MARY HAYS: I'll do it.

JOSEPH MARTIN: But you're a woman—

MARY HAYS: I've got two hands and a brain, don't I? Load the gun, Joseph.

JOSEPH MARTIN: Yes, ma'am.

10 Easy-to-Read American History Plays • Scholastic Professional Books © 2001

TEACHING GUIDE

Background

After Lexington and Concord, the colonies faced many obstacles. They had to establish a new government and build an army. The Americans had no navy, while the British ruled the seas. Many colonists, some of them wealthy, remained loyal to England. Some merchants, more concerned with profit than patriotism, sold American goods to the British army. The Continental Congress didn't have the right to tax the colonists, so raising money to fight the war was always a problem. And finally, the 13 colonies often squabbled with one another.

The colonies did have some advantages. Americans were fighting on familiar territory, and for their own freedom. British soldiers, far from home, were less invested in the outcome of the war. The war stretched from Maine to Georgia and for 300 miles inland. No matter how professional the British soldiers were, they couldn't be everywhere at once. When America declared its independence from England in 1776, foreign countries felt that they could then help the new country.

Early in the war, the British hoped to use military might to cut off New England from the rest of the colonies, but they failed. In 1776 and 1777 Washington and his troops were unable to keep the British from taking New York City and then the capital, Philadelphia. Undersupplied and demoralized, the Americans spent a hard winter at Valley Forge. Baron von Steuben arrived from Germany, and with his help the Americans became well-trained soldiers. In the spring of 1778, France announced its support for the colonies, sending additional money, supplies, and soldiers.

The war effectively ended in 1781 when the Americans surrounded Cornwallis and his British troops at Yorktown, Virginia. In 1783 the two countries finally signed a peace treaty.

Vocabulary
Some readers may not be familiar with the following words:

artillery: large guns that are too heavy to carry

barber: someone who cuts hair

canteen: something people use to carry water when they go on a hike or a march

headquarters: the main place for the people in charge of something

laundry: clothes that need to be, or have been, washed

private: person who has a low position in the army

Books to Build Interest

The Arrow Over the Door by Joseph Bruchac (Dial, 1998)

Molly Pitcher, Young Patriot by Augusta Stevenson (Aladdin, 1986)

The Winter of Red Snow: The Revolutionary Diary of Abigail Jane Stewart by Kristiana Gregory (Scholastic, 1996)

A Young Patriot: The American Revolution as Experienced by One Boy by Jim Murphy (Clarion, 1996)

Web Sites

http://www.geocities.com/Pentagon/Quarters/9769/mollyp.html (United States Field Artillery Association)

http://www.ushistory.org/valleyforge/ (Independence Hall Association)

10 Easy-to-Read American History Plays • Scholastic Professional Books © 2001

ACTIVITIES

Revolutionary Women

Women had an active part in the American Revolution. One woman, Margaret Corbin, took over a cannon when her husband was killed at Fort Washington in New York. She was wounded. Sybil Luddington made her own midnight ride to warn of approaching British troops. Deborah Sampson disguised herself as a man and fought as a soldier. Have students find out more about women's participation in the war. They may focus on a specific woman or take a broader view.

Where the Americans Met the British

The Battle of Monmouth was only one of many confrontations between American and British forces. Let pairs or groups of students choose one battle and report on it. Their reports may take a variety of forms—a reenactment of the battle with toy figures, a story map, a play, or diary entry, and so on. Students can present their reports in the order in which the battles occurred. Guide discussions before and after the presentations to help students understand the importance of each battle in the overall fight for freedom.

Will the Real Molly Pitcher Please Stand Up?

Like Paul Revere, Molly Pitcher has become an American folk hero, but little is really known about her. Private Joseph Martin wrote the only eyewitness account of Mary Hays's bravery at the Battle of Monmouth. Some sources give her husband's name as William, some as John. Explore other American female folk legends with students. Read aloud or make available stories from *Cut From the Same Cloth* by Robert D. San Souci (Philomel, 1993). Encourage students to create their own American Revolution female folk hero.

Benjamin Franklin in France

Thanks to the work of Benjamin Franklin, French King Louis XVI signed a treaty with the American colonies that recognized their independence. Students can visit the Franklin Institute Web site at http://sln.fi.edu/franklin to find out more about the contributions of Benjamin Franklin. Ask them to research one contribution and make a trading card about it. The card should feature a likeness of Franklin on the front, along with a title such as "Printer," "Inventor," or "Writer." On the back, students should write a brief fact about Franklin's accomplishment.

Chasing the British

Students can add to their map books with maps showing Valley Forge, Philadelphia, and the movement to Monmouth, and on to New York City. They can also highlight the battles of Brandywine and Germantown in Pennsylvania, and some may want to include the gravesite of Mary Hays at Carlisle, Pennsylvania.

Molly Memorial

"Commission" students to design a memorial to Molly Pitcher. Talk about memorial statues and plaques they may have seen, or that are in your community. Show examples of both representational and abstract designs for students to study. Their designs should include the text that will accompany the memorial.

10 Easy-to-Read American History Plays • Scholastic Professional Books © 2001

RIDING TO FREEDOM

The Underground Railroad (1793-1850)

Cast of Characters (in order of appearance)

"Big" Jim Hudson: *Southern farmer*

Rachel: *African-American enslaved woman*

Seth: *African-American enslaved man*

"Little" Jim Hudson: *"Big" Jim's grandson, also a farmer*

Pearl: *Rachel and Seth's granddaughter*

Charlie: *Pearl's husband*

John Parker: *Ex-slave, "conductor" on the Underground Railroad*

Parker: *Pearl and Charlie's daughter*

10 Easy-to-Read American History Plays • Scholastic Professional Books © 2001

★ ACT 1 ★

SCENE: SOUTHERN FARM, 1793

JIM HUDSON: Bess and Tom from Hugh Bell's farm ran off last night. I don't suppose you all know anything about that, do you?

RACHEL: No, sir.

SETH: No, I didn't hear a word about it.

JIM HUDSON: I didn't think so. You're not helping Bess and Tom by keeping quiet. They've got dogs chasing after them. They'll have to run through the swamp. If the dogs don't get them, then the alligators will.

RACHEL: Bess and Tom have two children. What happened to the children?

JIM HUDSON: They're gone, too, and Hugh Bell's plenty mad. If you know something, speak up. *(pause)* There's a new law. Even if Tom and Bess reach the North, Hugh Bell can send slave catchers up there after them. They can catch Tom and Bess and their children and bring them right back here.

SETH: They can bring back Tom and Bess if they make it to a free state—even if that state doesn't allow slavery?

JIM HUDSON: That's right. You think about that. You think about what Hugh Bell's going to do to Tom and Bess when he gets them back. I've never seen Hugh so mad in all my life.

RACHEL: You think he'll take the children away from Bess? You think he might sell them?

JIM HUDSON: I know so. If you know something, Rachel, say it now.

RACHEL: No, sir, I don't know anything.

JIM HUDSON: We know about your Underground Railroad. We know who the conductors are. We know where the stations are. You might run, but you won't be able to hide.

SETH: Then you know more than we do, Mr. Hudson. We don't know anything about a railroad.

JIM HUDSON: When Hugh Bell catches Tom and Bess, I won't be able to do a thing to help them. It'll be too late then.

RACHEL: Seth's right, Mr. Hudson. We don't know anything.

JIM HUDSON: I don't believe you, not for a minute. Get on back to work—and don't even think about running away yourselves. You don't want me chasing after you all.

(Jim Hudson leaves.)

10 Easy-to-Read American History Plays • Scholastic Professional Books © 2001

SETH: I told you it was too dangerous. They know everything. They'll track us down.

RACHEL: Next time our conductor comes around, I'm riding to freedom on that Underground Railroad. You can come with me, or you can stay here, but I'm taking the children and going.

➤ ACT 2 ➤

SCENE 1: OUTSIDE THE HUDSON FARMHOUSE, 1850

"LITTLE" JIM HUDSON: I don't have any money. The bank won't give me any to buy some seeds. I don't have any choice. I've got to sell this place.

PEARL: You mean you've got to sell us.

CHARLIE: I'm not letting my family get split up.

"LITTLE" JIM HUDSON: I'll do what I can to keep you all together, but I can't promise. I need the money.

PEARL: We've worked hard for your family for over 60 years. You could find a good home for us—for all of us.

"LITTLE" JIM HUDSON: "Big" Jim spoiled you all. Don't you understand? You don't get to say what happens to you.

CHARLIE: How can we forget?

"LITTLE" JIM HUDSON: Don't get smart with me. Now, go on, get back to work.

("Little" Jim starts to walk away but then stops.)

"LITTLE" JIM HUDSON: Go get your baby and bring her to the house.

PEARL: Why?

"LITTLE" JIM HUDSON: I'm keeping her with me, right by my side, every second of the day, just in case you're thinking of running away. I know you wouldn't leave without your baby.

CHARLIE: I'm not going to let you do that.

"LITTLE" JIM HUDSON: Do you want me to sell you right now, Charlie? I could. Now, go get your baby.

("Little" Jim walks away.)

CHARLIE: What are we going to do? We're supposed to leave tonight!

PEARL: That's it. I'm not leaving.

10 Easy-to-Read American History Plays • Scholastic Professional Books © 2001

SCENE 2: OUTSIDE THE HUDSON FARMHOUSE, LATER THAT NIGHT

(A bird cries in the woods.)

CHARLIE: That's it! That's the signal!

PEARL: I'm not going. I mean it.

(John Parker seems to appear out of nowhere.)

JOHN PARKER: Train's ready to leave the station. Better get on board.

PEARL: He's got our baby in there. He's put her right at the foot of his bed. He knows I won't go without my baby.

CHARLIE: If I can't figure out how to get my baby out of there, I'm not going either.

JOHN PARKER: The boss man—does he sleep deep or light?

PEARL: I don't know. He snores.

JOHN PARKER: Tell me about the inside of the house. Where's his bedroom? What kind of furniture has he got in there and where is it? Tell me everything.

CHARLIE: What are you going to do?

JOHN PARKER: You'll see.

SCENE 3: OUTSIDE "LITTLE" JIM'S BEDROOM WINDOW, AN HOUR LATER

(Charlie looks through the window.)

PEARL: Tell me what's going on.

CHARLIE: "Little" Jim's sleeping. The baby's at the foot of the bed.

PEARL: Is she all right?

CHARLIE: I think so. There's a candle and a gun on the table beside the bed—

PEARL: What is it?

CHARLIE: John Parker just opened the door . . . oh, no!

PEARL: What?

CHARLIE: "Little" Jim just turned over . . . No, it's okay. He's asleep . . . John's taking off his shoes . . . he's crawling over to the bed—he's got the baby! He's got the baby! Run, Pearl! Run!

(Charlie and Pearl run away.)

"LITTLE" JIM HUDSON *(shouting from inside the bedroom):* You better stop right now!

(There is a sound in the bedroom of a table falling over. John Parker runs outside the house holding the baby. A few seconds later, "Little" Jim runs out after him.)

"LITTLE" JIM HUDSON: You'll never make it! I'll find you! I'll hunt you down—see if I don't!

➤ ACT 3 ➤

THE LIVING ROOM OF A HOUSE IN CANADA, 1855

PARKER: And then what happened?

PEARL: Well, we ran down to the river. John Parker had a boat down there.

CHARLIE: Pretty soon he came tearing down to the river with you in his arms.

PEARL: But "Little" Jim was shooting at us. John made all of us lie down in the bottom of the boat.

CHARLIE: Then he rowed and rowed and rowed like his arms were machines.

PEARL: He got us to the other side of the river. "Little" Jim didn't have a boat, so he couldn't come after us right then. Well, he did try to swim after us, but he didn't get very far.

CHARLIE: Then John took us to another conductor on the Underground Railroad.

PEARL: A lot of other people helped us to get here to Canada.

PARKER: And now we help other people.

CHARLIE: That's right. Our house is one of the last stops on the Underground Railroad.

(There's a knock at the door.)

PEARL: Who is it?

WOMAN: A friend told me to follow the North Star, and I'd find your house.

(Pearl opens the door.)

PEARL: Come in. We've been waiting for you.

10 Easy-to-Read American History Plays • Scholastic Professional Books © 2001

TEACHING GUIDE

Background

Slavery began in America in 1619 when a Dutch ship and an English ship captured a Spanish ship carrying 100 enslaved Africans. The Dutch ship returned to Jamestown with about 20 Africans who were put to work in the tobacco fields. The birth of the abolition movement occurred over a hundred years later, in 1775, when Benjamin Franklin established the first abolitionist society in America.

Never a formal organization, the Underground Railroad probably began after the passage of the Fugitive Slave Act of 1793. The act made it illegal to help fugitive slaves and also allowed slaveholders or hired slave catchers to capture runaway slaves, even if they had reached free states. Using a code based on railroad terminology, slaves traveled to northern states or into Canada or south into Spanish Florida or Mexico by land or water. "Conductors" led their "passengers" or "freight" to "stations" (safe houses) along the lines (routes). The heaviest concentration of traffic was in Pennsylvania, Ohio, Indiana, New York, and New England.

In 1808 Congress stopped the importation of enslaved Africans into the United States. However, many people were still smuggled into the country. As states joined the new union, it had to be determined whether they would be free states where slavery was outlawed, or slave states. To maintain the balance of free and slave states, the Missouri Compromise of 1820, the Compromise of 1850, and the Kansas-Nebraska Act were implemented. The Compromise of 1850 contained another, harsher, Fugitive Slave Act.

With the outbreak of the Civil War in 1861, the Underground Railroad shut down. It's estimated that anywhere from 40,000 to 100,000 enslaved Africans escaped to freedom using the Underground Railroad.

Vocabulary Some readers may not be familiar with the following words:

conductor: ticket-taker on a train or bus

spoiled: overprotected

station: regular stopping place on a route

swamp: wet, marshy land

Books to Build Interest

Aunt Harriet's Underground Railroad in the Sky by Faith Ringgold (Crown, 1994)

Get On Board: The Story of the Underground Railroad by Jim Haskins (Scholastic, 1993)

Many Thousands Gone by Virginia Hamilton (Econo-Clad Books, 1999)

The Underground Railroad by Raymond Bial (Houghton Mifflin, 1995)

Web Sites

http://www.cr.nps.gov (National Park Service)

http://www.education.ucdavis.edu/NEW/STC/lesson/socstud/railroad (University of California at Davis Department of Education)

ACTIVITIES

The Route of the Underground Railroad

Enslaved African Americans in the South used escape routes to the North and into Canada. They also fled into Mexico and what was then Spanish Florida. Students can create maps of the Underground Railroad for their books of American history maps. Encourage them to choose a route on their map and imagine a trip made on it in the past. Students can write diary entries or include captions on their maps that tell about the imaginary trip.

All Aboard! Conductors on the Underground Railroad

Harriet Tubman and Frederick Douglass traveled along the Underground Railroad to freedom. Tubman returned to the South several times as a conductor. Another conductor, John Fairfield, was formerly a slaveholder. Because he was white, he was able to travel in the South posing as a slave trader. He "bought" slaves and then took them North where they would be free. Conductor John Parker really did snatch a couple's baby from the foot of a plantation owner's bed. Ask students to find out more about a conductor on the Underground Railroad. They can write poems, songs, biographies, or plays to immortalize that person's contributions.

About Abolitionists

In 1775 Benjamin Franklin started the first abolitionist society in the United States. The society of Quakers were also active abolitionists. Have students create an Abolitionists' Hall of Fame. They should include a variety of abolitionists—black, white, male, female, Northern, and Southern. Students can draw portraits of the abolitionists or locate photographs, and write accounts of their activities.

What's the Word?

It was forbidden for most enslaved people to learn to read or write. Communication about the Underground Railroad was verbal, often sung in spirituals. In addition, the Underground Railroad had its own set of code words that used railroad terminology such as "conductors" and "passengers." After students research the code words used on the Underground Railroad, challenge them to expand the code with additional words and hand gestures.

The Drinking Gourd and Other Constellations

African Americans escaping from the South often used the constellation the Big Dipper to guide their way. They were often urged to "follow the drinking gourd." If there's a planetarium nearby, arrange a visit for your class. You might also find out if there is a local astronomy or stargazers' club in your community; if so, invite one of their members to speak to the class about constellations. Encourage students to find out more about the "drinking gourd" or other constellations. They may draw star maps and/or retell myths about the constellations.

Patching Together the Story

Quilts were sometimes used to convey directions for routes of escape. Share examples with students from the adult trade book *Hidden in Plain Sight: A Secret Story of Quilts and the Underground Railroad* by Jacqueline L. Tobin and Raymond G. Dobard, Ph.D. (Bantam Doubleday Dell, 2000) or in the children's book *Sweet Harriet and the Freedom Quilt* by Deborah Hopkinson (Random House, 1995). Let each student create a panel on a sheet of paper for an Underground Railroad quilt. Provide a variety of art materials for them to use. Piece together the quilt on one wall.

10 Easy-to-Read American History Plays • Scholastic Professional Books © 2001

THE COUNTRY TORN APART

The Civil War (1861-1865)

Cast of Characters (in order of appearance)

Narrator

Faye Blaire: *A woman living in South Carolina, a Southerner*

Miles Green: *Faye's cousin living in Washington, D.C., a Northerner*

Jess Blaire: *Faye's husband, a Southerner*

William Henry Seward: *Secretary of State*

Abraham Lincoln: *President of the United States*

Newspaper Reporter

Phil Sheridan: *Union army officer*

General Robert E. Lee: *Leader of the Confederate army*

General Ulysses S. Grant: *Leader of the Union army*

⚊ ACT 1 • Shots Fired at Fort Sumter ⚊

NARRATOR: The Republican Party began in 1854. The party wanted to fight the spread of slavery in new states and territories of the United States. In 1860, Republican Abraham Lincoln was elected president. The Southern states of South Carolina, Mississippi, Florida, Alabama, Georgia, Louisiana, and Texas seceded, or left, the Union.

SCENE: FAYE BLAIRE'S HOUSE IN CHARLESTON, SOUTH CAROLINA, APRIL 12, 1861

FAYE BLAIRE: Nobody wants a war. Nobody here is really happy that the Southern states left the Union.

MILES GREEN: I must say, nobody in the North seems to care that the South did secede.

FAYE BLAIRE: I think President Lincoln minds very much. I think he would do almost anything to try to keep the country together.

MILES GREEN: He certainly won't let slavery spread to new states.

FAYE BLAIRE: No, but it seems to be all right with Mr. Lincoln if the South continues to have slavery.

MILES GREEN: The North needs your cotton so our factories can make shirts and dresses.

FAYE BLAIRE: It takes a lot of work to raise enough cotton to make all those shirts and dresses. If Mr. Lincoln frees the slaves, who will work in the fields?

MILES GREEN: You sound like you think slavery's all right.

FAYE BLAIRE: I don't. I think slavery's a horrible thing. But South Carolina is my home now. What can I do? My husband and children are here. My friends are here.

MILES GREEN: You and your family could come and stay with us.

FAYE BLAIRE: You worry too much. It won't come to war.

MILES GREEN: You'd better hope not. There are more people in the North than in the South. Most of the factories and railroads are in the North.

(Jess Blaire comes in, looking very serious.)

FAYE BLAIRE: Jess, what is it?

JESS BLAIRE: Lincoln is sending supplies to Fort Sumter.

MILES GREEN: He's not going to give up the forts here without a fight. They belong to the federal government—and that's the North now.

JESS BLAIRE: If a fort's on Confederate land, it belongs to the South now. *Our* president Jefferson Davis isn't going to let Northern ships and supplies in here.

FAYE BLAIRE: There'll be a war.

10 Easy-to-Read American History Plays • Scholastic Professional Books © 2001

(They hear the sound of guns firing in Charleston harbor.)

MILES GREEN: There *is* a war.

JESS BLAIRE: Miles, you'd better pack your bags. I don't know what's going to happen. You'd better get back to Washington while you can.

MILES GREEN: When will I see you again?

FAYE BLAIRE: I don't know. I don't know.

➤ ACT 2 • Emancipation Proclamation ➤

NARRATOR: The Confederate army fired on Fort Sumter and took it a few days later. The Civil War had begun. Lincoln called for 75,000 men to join the Union army. Jefferson Davis called for 100,000 men to join the Confederate army. Men on both sides rushed to join.

SCENE 1: THE WHITE HOUSE, JULY, 1862

WILLIAM HENRY SEWARD: You can't. You can't free the slaves in the South now.

ABRAHAM LINCOLN: I can, and I will free them. That's one of the reasons we're fighting this war.

WILLIAM HENRY SEWARD: We just lost at Bull Creek. The Confederates beat us badly. If you free the slaves now, it will look like we need their help to win this war. It'll look like we want them to rise up and fight.

ABRAHAM LINCOLN: The abolitionists keep asking me what I'm going to do about slavery. They may not keep supporting the war if I don't do something.

WILLIAM HENRY SEWARD: Just wait until the North wins a big victory. That's all I'm asking you to do—just wait a few more months. We'll win soon.

ABRAHAM LINCOLN: All right, I'll wait. But after our next victory, I'm going to free the slaves in the South.

SCENE 2: NEWSPAPER OFFICE IN WASHINGTON, D.C., SEPTEMBER 22, 1862

NEWSPAPER REPORTER: Wow! News is pouring out of Washington! We just had a big win at Antietam *and* Lincoln just freed the slaves!

MILES GREEN: When? What did he say?

NEWSPAPER REPORTER: He said that if the Southern states didn't come back to the Union by the end of the year, then all the slaves living there would be free.

MILES GREEN: That's not going to make any of the Southern states come back. And they're sure not going to let the slaves go free because Lincoln says to.

NEWSPAPER REPORTER: He's the president, isn't he? He had to say *something* about slavery, didn't he? Now the world knows what the fight's about—slavery.

MILES GREEN: Not everybody in the South is a slaveholder. My cousin and her husband don't own anybody—

NEWSPAPER REPORTER: Did they speak out against it? Did they try to stop it?

MILES GREEN: No, but—

NEWSPAPER REPORTER: Did they leave the South and move up North?

MILES GREEN: Would you do it? Would you be able to give up everything—your home, your family, your friends—and leave?

NEWSPAPER REPORTER: I like to think I would.

MILES GREEN: I haven't heard from my cousin in over three months. I don't even know if she and her family are still alive.

NEWSPAPER REPORTER: This war's tearing everybody apart. Look at Lincoln and his wife. She's from the South. I hear her brothers are fighting in the Confederate army.

MILES GREEN: I wonder what she thinks about Lincoln freeing the slaves?

➤ ACT 3 • Surrender at Appomattox ➤

NARRATOR: None of the Southern states returned to the Union. Despite the Emancipation Proclamation, the slaves in the South weren't freed. The Civil War wore on for four long and bloody years at places like Shiloh, Gettysburg, and Vicksburg. In April of 1865, the Union army took the Confederate capital of Richmond, Virginia. The war was over.

SCENE 1: APPOMATTOX, VIRGINIA, APRIL 9, 1865

(Dressed in his finest uniform and carrying his sword, Lee rides in.)

PHIL SHERIDAN: General Lee, I'm Philip Sheridan. It's an honor to meet you. General Grant will be here very soon. Why don't you come inside with me?

GENERAL LEE: Thank you, sir. Could you see to it that my horse, Traveler, is watered and fed?

PHIL SHERIDAN: Certainly, sir. He's a fine animal.

GENERAL LEE: He saved my life more than once on the battlefield.

(Lee goes inside the small stone house. After a few seconds, Grant rides up. His uniform is torn and muddy.)

GENERAL GRANT: Is he here yet?

PHIL SHERIDAN: He's inside. He looks a whole lot better than you do.

GENERAL GRANT: I just came from the battlefield. I didn't have time to change. I don't mean any disrespect.

10 Easy-to-Read American History Plays • Scholastic Professional Books © 2001

PHIL SHERIDAN: Did you know Lee when you were at West Point?

GENERAL GRANT: No, but I met him in Mexico when we were fighting down there. He wouldn't let me into General Scott's tent because I was too dirty.

PHIL SHERIDAN: Do you think he'll remember you?

GENERAL GRANT: I don't think General Lee will ever forget me.

SCENE 2: INSIDE WILMER MCLEAN'S HOUSE AT APPOMATTOX, A FEW MINUTES LATER

GENERAL GRANT: I'm sorry I'm late, General Lee.

GENERAL LEE: I guess we have a few loose ends to tie up.

GENERAL GRANT: Yes, sir, we do. I've talked to President Lincoln. Here's what he wants from you and your men. All your men are to be set free. Your officers get to keep their horses.

GENERAL LEE: Many of my soldiers own their own horses and mules. They should be able to keep those. They'll need the animals to help them put in new crops.

GENERAL GRANT: That's no problem.

GENERAL LEE: I do have a favor to ask for my men. They're very hungry. Could you provide them with some food and water?

GENERAL GRANT: Certainly, sir.

(Lee and Grant stand up and shake hands.)

GENERAL LEE: I won't say it's been a pleasure, General Grant, but you and your army fought well.

GENERAL GRANT: It's not a happy day for any of us, General Lee. I'm glad this war is over.

SCENE 3: NEWSPAPER OFFICE IN WASHINGTON, D.C., LATER THAT DAY

NEWSPAPER REPORTER: Hey, cheer up! The war's over! We're one, big, happy country again!

MILES GREEN: I finally heard from my cousin.

NEWSPAPER REPORTER: That's good, right? You heard from her. That means she's alive.

MILES GREEN: Her husband died at Lookout Mountain. He was a good man.

NEWSPAPER REPORTER: A lot of good men on both sides died. They say over 600,000 soldiers died and almost 400,000 were hurt—and that's not counting ordinary people who died.

MILES GREEN: I hope we learned a lesson from this. Lincoln was right—a house divided against itself cannot stand.

10 Easy-to-Read American History Plays • Scholastic Professional Books © 2001

TEACHING GUIDE

Background

Many differences separated the North and the South. The North relied on manufacturing and industry while the South's economy was based on agriculture which depended upon slave labor. Each region interpreted the Constitution differently. The North wanted a federal government with some power—the ability to build, maintain, and improve systems, such as transportation. The South favored a stricter reading of the Constitution wherein states held more authority than the federal government. With the opening of the West, the division between the North and South grew sharper. The South wanted these lands to be open to slavery; the North wanted to outlaw slavery there. With more and more free states entering the Union, the South feared that slavery would soon be prohibited in the United States. The final blow came when Republican Abraham Lincoln was elected president in 1860. South Carolina, Mississippi, Florida, Alabama, Georgia, Louisiana, and Texas seceded.

At first, Lincoln hoped to preserve the Union, but all compromises failed. The war began at Fort Sumter, South Carolina, in April 1861, when Confederates began firing on the fort. South Carolina said that the fort belonged to the Confederacy, but federal troops still occupied it and Lincoln was sending more supplies to them. After Fort Sumter, both sides scrambled to build their armies. At Bull Run, the first major battle of the war, the Confederates beat the Union soldiers. In the following year, 1862, each side tried to capture its opponent's capital—the North aimed for Richmond, Virginia, and the South headed for Washington, D.C. A series of Northern defeats was offset by a win at Antietam. The victory gave Lincoln the impetus he needed to issue the Emancipation Proclamation which freed the slaves in the Southern states.

In 1862, Northern commander David Farragut captured New Orleans. In 1863, Lee and his army were defeated at Gettysburg. Soon the last Confederate fort on the Mississippi had been taken. Ulysses S. Grant was appointed head of the Union army in March 1864. General William T. Sherman began his march through Georgia. On April 1, 1865, Lee had to abandon the capital, Richmond. He surrendered to Grant on April 9 at Appomattox, Virginia. Five days later, Lincoln was assassinated.

Vocabulary
Some readers may not be familiar with the following words:

disrespect: without respect

emancipation: the act of setting free from slavery

ordinary: usual

proclamation: public announcement

secede: to break away

surrender: to give up

territories: lands ruled by a country or state

uniform: set of clothes worn by people in a certain group

union: people joined together

Books to Build Interest

A House Divided: The Lives of Ulysses S. Grant and Robert E. Lee by Jules Archer (Scholastic, 1996)

Pink and Say by Patricia Polacco (Putnam, 1994)

Scholastic Encyclopedia of the Civil War by Catherine Clinton (Scholastic, 1999)

Silent Thunder by Andrea Davis Pinkney (Hyperion, 1999)

When Will This Cruel War Be Over? by Barry Denenberg (Scholastic, 1996)

Web Sites

http://www.net.ins.net/showcase/creative/lincoln.html (Abraham Lincoln Online)

http://www.sunsite.utk.edu/civil-war/warweb.html (University of Tennessee)

10 Easy-to-Read American History Plays • Scholastic Professional Books © 2001

ACTIVITIES

Southern Names/Northern Names

Different names were often given to the same Civil War battles. Northerners tended to name battles after nearby bodies of water; Southerners used the name of locations on land. For instance, the same battle was called the Battle of Bull Run by the North, and the Battle of Manassas by the South. Have students research an important battle of the Civil War. They can find out both names, why the battle was important, what happened, and then make a map of it to add to their map book. Students may also want to re-create an enactment of the battle using their maps or other props.

Opposite Sides

In the play the cousins Faye Blaire and Miles Green are on opposite sides of the war. Tell students to think of an issue about which they feel strongly. Then ask them to consider the other side of the issue. See if students can suspend their own opinions and "walk around in someone else's shoes" for a while. Talk about whether or not the experience changed their original opinions.

Civil War Firsts

The Civil War was the first American war to be photographed. Mathew Brady's photos bring the war to life for us today. The ships *Monitor* and *Merrimack* were the first ironclad ships to be used in battle. Challenge students to research Civil War "firsts" and report about them.

The Blue and Gray (and Butternut)

Under all the mud, General Grant's uniform at Appomattox was blue. General Lee wore a gray uniform. Some Confederate soldiers dressed in uniforms the color of butternut squash. Encourage students to find out more about the different kinds of Union and Confederate uniforms. They may draw the uniforms or design a set of paper dolls. Some students may want to create uniforms for dolls or themselves.

Civil War Notables

Create a Civil War Wall of Fame in your classroom. Let students design posters for a variety of people involved in the Civil War including soldiers, politicians, spies, nurses, civilians, writers, and photographers. If possible, have students write brief biographies of the notables and tape-record them. Play the audiotape to share with parents or other students who visit the classroom.

Civil War Time Capsule

What do students think is important to remember about the Civil War? What things would they tell future generations about that event? Suggest that students make Civil War time capsules. Provide empty containers such as oatmeal containers or cereal boxes to groups of students. They can fill the containers with meaningful items about the war such as copies of diary entries, photographs, songs, maps, descriptions of battles, and speeches. Students can share their time capsules with other classes. What did the other classes learn from the time capsules?

10 Easy-to-Read American History Plays • Scholastic Professional Books © 2001

"DONE"

The Transcontinental Railroad (1859-1869)

Cast of Characters (in order of appearance)

Narrator

Senator

Theodore Judah: *Railroad engineer*

Leland Stanford: *Head of the Central Pacific (CP) Railroad*

Charles Crocker: *Head of the CP Railroad*

Thomas Durant: *Head of the Union Pacific (UP) Railroad*

Sean Casey: *Worker on the UP Railroad*

James Murphy: *Worker on the UP Railroad*

Sam Chen: *Worker on the CP Railroad*

Ang Luke: *Worker on the CP Railroad*

Crowd 1–10

10 Easy-to-Read American History Plays • Scholastic Professional Books © 2001

◄ ACT 1 ►

SCENE 1: WASHINGTON, D.C., 1859

NARRATOR: In 1859 Theodore Judah traveled to Washington, D.C. He wanted to talk members of Congress into building a transcontinental railroad—a railroad that stretched across the United States.

SENATOR: Listen, you can't build a railroad from California to the East. There are mountains in the way. Why, some of them are over 12,000 feet high.

THEODORE JUDAH: We'll go through the mountains. We'll blast tunnels through them.

SENATOR: You know how much that would cost? Listen, the Congress doesn't have that much money—even if the other senators wanted to give it to you. Don't count on me to vote for this wild idea of yours.

THEODORE JUDAH: California is a rich state. A railroad that joins the eastern and the western parts of the United States will make lots of money.

SENATOR: Listen, some of the southern states are saying they're going to quit the U.S. There might be a war. We can't waste time talking about a railroad.

THEODORE JUDAH: If the southern states do quit and there is a civil war, then the northern states will need California on its side. You can use the railroad to send gold and silver to the North.

SENATOR: Listen, if California's such a rich state, then go back there and get the money for your railroad.

THEODORE JUDAH: I guess I will.

SCENE 2: SACRAMENTO, CALIFORNIA, 1864

NARRATOR: Judah talked some rich California businessmen, including Leland Stanford and Charles Crocker, into starting the Central Pacific Railroad. Then the Civil War broke out, and Congress decided it was important to have a transcontinental railroad. The Central Pacific Railroad started building east from Sacramento, California.

LELAND STANFORD: It's kind of sad, isn't it? Judah died after sailing to Panama and then traveling through the jungle there to catch another boat.

CHARLES CROCKER: Yes it is sad, but until our railroad's built, that's the fastest way to travel from California to the East.

LELAND STANFORD: We've only laid about 18 miles of track in over a year. We're about to run out of supplies and workers and money.

CHARLES CROCKER: I've got an idea about workers. Let's hire Chinese men. They work hard—and we can pay them less than we pay our other workers.

10 Easy-to-Read American History Plays • Scholastic Professional Books © 2001

LELAND STANFORD: I don't know . . .

CHARLES CROCKER: Are you going out there to lay track yourself?

LELAND STANFORD: Are you kidding?

CHARLES CROCKER: All right then. We either hire you or the Chinese. Which is it going to be?

SCENE 3: OMAHA, NEBRASKA, 1865

NARRATOR: The Union Pacific Railroad started building tracks west from Omaha, Nebraska. They weren't having much more luck than the Central Pacific.

THOMAS DURANT: How's it going, men?

SEAN CASEY: All right if you don't mind digging in a little mud.

JAMES MURPHY: A little mud?! I'm up to my knees in mud!

THOMAS DURANT: Good! Good! Keep up the good work!

(Durant walks on.)

SEAN CASEY: I see that he keeps his feet nice and dry.

JAMES MURPHY: And clean.

SEAN CASEY: I just hope we get paid on time this week.

(Sean and James go back to work.)

THOMAS DURANT: What am I going to do? The Union Pacific started laying tracks over a year ago, and we haven't even gotten out of Omaha yet! We don't have any workers. We don't have any money to pay workers. But the war might be over soon. All those soldiers will need jobs. That's it! The war'll be over soon—but there aren't any trees on the Great Plains. We need trees for the tracks. Where are we going to get the wood? We'll have to buy it. That's going to cost a fortune.

SCENE 4: CAPE HORN, CALIFORNIA, 1865

NARRATOR: Chinese men proved to be good workers. The Central Pacific gave them the job of blasting a ledge along a 4,000-foot-high cliff called Cape Horn. A man would be lowered in a basket down a cliff. He would pack explosives in the cliff and then be pulled back up.

SAM CHEN: They had better be paying attention up there. When I give the signal, they better pull me up before this stuff explodes.

ANG LUKE: Before I get in my basket, I always tell them, "The signal is *not* the explosion. If you hear the explosion, and you haven't pulled me up the cliff yet, then you've missed my signal."

10 Easy-to-Read American History Plays • Scholastic Professional Books © 2001

SAM CHEN: I had to write to Wang's family in China and tell them he was killed.

ANG LUKE: He had four children, too. He was going back to China after we made it through the mountains. He sent almost all the money he made back to his family.

SAM CHEN: Don't talk about families. It makes me miss my own wife and children. You're lucky you're not married yet.

ANG LUKE: There aren't any women around for hundreds and hundreds of miles. Who am I going to marry?

SAM CHEN: I'm done.

ANG LUKE: Don't signal yet. This hole isn't big enough. I've got to find another one to put the explosives in.

(There is the sound of a loud explosion. Both men hang on to their baskets.)

SAM CHEN: That was too soon!

ANG LUKE: That was too close!

SAM CHEN: Another family in China's going to get a sad letter.

▬ ACT 2 ▬

SCENE: UTAH, APRIL 28, 1869

NARRATOR: Charles Crocker wanted to get some attention for the Central Pacific Railroad. He promised that his workers would lay 10 miles of track in one day. Before that, the record was 8 miles in one day.

CHARLES CROCKER: You're the Central Pacific's best workers! Don't let me down! Remember—you'll get four days' pay today—if you complete 10 miles of track!

SAM CHEN: This is better than blowing up mountains! I'll do this any day!

ANG LUKE: Tell me that *after* we've laid 10 miles of track.

CHARLES CROCKER: That's right, men! Move those spikes and bolts and rails to the crew! Faster! Faster! One mile an hour—we can do it!

SAM CHEN: "We" can do it?

ANG LUKE: Sure—we—you and me. Crocker's busy telling us what to do.

CHARLES CROCKER: You, Irish! Put down those rails and spike them into place! Keep it moving! Keep it moving!

SAM CHEN: I bet the Union Pacific workers aren't working this hard today.

10 Easy-to-Read American History Plays • Scholastic Professional Books © 2001

ANG LUKE: They don't need to. I heard they're about 9 miles from Promontory Summit. That's where the tracks are meeting.

CHARLES CROCKER: Good job, men! We've laid 6 miles of track! Take a break for lunch! Take an hour!

SAM CHEN: Do you think he'll let us take a nap, too?

ANG LUKE: No, but I bet he takes one.

CHARLES CROCKER: We're almost there, men! Lift those hammers! Hammer those spikes! Think of the newspaper headlines! Soon everyone in America will be reading about what we did today!

SAM CHEN: What "we" did today?

ANG LUKE: Sure—you and me—we. What are you going to do with the extra pay?

SAM CHEN: I'm going to take it back to China. It's too hot and dry here.

(A train whistle sounds.)

CHARLES CROCKER: We did it! We did it! We laid 10 miles and 56 feet of tracks in 12 hours! That's a record! We used 25,800 ties; 3,520 rails; 28,160 spikes; and 14,080 bolts! We lifted over 2,000,000 pounds of metal today!

SAM CHEN: No wonder I'm so tired.

ANG LUKE: We may be tired, but we're richer.

⟶ ACT 3 ⟵

PROMONTORY SUMMIT, UTAH, MAY 10, 1869

NARRATOR: Finally, the Central Pacific and Union Pacific railroads met in Utah. Two trains, one from the East and one from the West, rolled up to each other. Then it was time to hammer in the last spike on the transcontinental railroad.

LELAND STANFORD: Ladies and gentleman! The last spike goes in!

(Stanford swings a sledgehammer and misses the spike. The crowd laughs and whistles.)

THOMAS DURANT: I guess it's up to the Union Pacific to finish the last track.

(Durant takes the hammer, swings, and misses. The crowd laughs and whistles.)

SAM CHEN: We'd still be in Sacramento and Omaha if those two had actually worked on the railroad.

SEAN CASEY: They aren't any better at paying their workers on time than they are with that hammer.

10 Easy-to-Read American History Plays • Scholastic Professional Books © 2001

ANG LUKE: I'm just glad to be here.

JAMES MURPHY: You weren't one of those basket men, were you?

ANG LUKE: Yes, and I made my own basket, too.

SEAN CASEY: No kidding?

SAM CHEN: Are you Irish? Yes? Are you going back to Ireland?

JAMES MURPHY: No, we thought we'd try our luck in California.

ANG LUKE: Now you can take the train.

SEAN CASEY: I worked too hard on that iron horse. I don't want to get anywhere near a train. I'm going to buy myself a real horse and head west. What about you two?

SAM CHEN: I'm going to open a restaurant at the train station in Green River, Wyoming. Ang's going back to China.

NARRATOR: An operator tapped three dots in Morse code on the telegraph when the spike was hammered in. People had gathered at telegraph offices to hear that message—"done." All across America, they cheered and celebrated.

TEACHING GUIDE

Background

Before the transcontinental railroad was built, people had to travel from the east coast to the west coast by ship. They had to cross the jungles of the Isthmus of Panama on foot or on horseback, and then board another ship to the west coast. Building a railroad across the Sierra Nevada Mountains seemed to be an impossible task. After years of exploring the mountains, engineer Thomas Judah found a route. Between 1856 and 1859 he tried to convince Congress to approve funds for a transcontinental railroad, but he was refused. Judah returned to California and formed the Central Pacific Railroad Company to build the railroad with private money. The Big Four—California businessmen Leland Stanford, Collis Huntington, Charles Crocker, and Mark Hopkins—invested in the new venture.

With the outbreak of the Civil War, the transcontinental railroad became what Lincoln called "a political as well as a military necessity." Congress passed the Pacific Railway Act in 1862. The Union Pacific Railroad was to build west from Omaha, Nebraska, and the Central Pacific Railroad would build east from Sacramento, California. Each railroad received the following amounts from Congress for each mile of track laid: $16,000 on the plains, $32,000 in the Great Basin, and $48,000 through the mountains. They also received sections of public land on each side of the tracks—a total of 33 million acres.

Irish immigrants formed the core of the Union Pacific's work force. Chinese men working for the Central Pacific Railroad blasted 15 tunnels through the Sierra Nevadas. They were sometimes able to lay only about eight inches of track a day. But on April 28, 1869, Chinese and Irish laborers laid ten miles of Central Pacific track in one day.

The two railroads met at Promontory Summit in Utah on May 10, 1869.

Vocabulary
Some readers may not be familiar with the following words:

engineer: person who uses science to plan and build buildings and roads

explosives: something that can explode

ledge: narrow shelf on a cliff

operator: person who uses a machine

telegraph: way to send messages by code

vote: to choose a plan or idea

Books to Build Interest

Death of the Iron Horse by Paul Goble (Aladdin, 1993)

The Iron Dragon Never Sleeps by Stephen Krensky (Yearling, 1995)

The Journal of Sean Sullivan by William Durbin (Scholastic, 1999)

Ten-Mile Day by Mary Ann Fraser (Henry Holt, 1996)

Web Sites

http://CPRR.org (Central Pacific Railroad)

http://www.uprr.com (Union Pacific Railroad)

10 Easy-to-Read American History Plays • Scholastic Professional Books © 2001

ACTIVITIES

Morse Code

The last iron spike to be driven into the transcontinental railroad and the sledgehammer used to strike it were wired so the sound could be telegraphed to the rest of the country. Since both Stanford and Durant swung and missed the spike, a telegraph operator named Shilling used Morse code to transmit the word *done*. Have students find out more about Morse code and send their own messages to each other.

Cattle Drives

To supply workers with meat as they worked in Wyoming, the Union Pacific Railroad got cattle from Charles Goodnight. He herded the cattle up from Texas on the Goodnight-Loving trail. Encourage groups of students to learn more about cattle drives and trails such as the Chisholm, the Goodnight-Loving, and the Shawnee. Each group can make a map of a trail and report on what a day on a cattle drive would be like. Explore with students how railroads affected cattle drives.

Rushing Across the Country—by Pony and Camel

Students may be familiar with express mail from the post office and private companies such as Federal Express. Define the word *express* for students as a company that is in business to carry goods, valuables, and money to their destinations in a safe and quick way. Express in the United States has taken many forms—messages carried under beaver hats between Boston and New York, the Pony Express, and the American Camel Express. Have pairs of students find out more about how express mail has been moved across the country. They can present their findings in short skits or two-person dialogues; one student wants to send something valuable across the country and the other student works for the express company. What kind of information would be important?

Build Your Own Railroad

Several different routes for the transcontinental railroad were considered. Geography and politics helped decide which route was eventually chosen. Give physical maps of the United States to groups of students. Assign the task of choosing the best route for a railroad to cross the country. It may begin and end at any city on the east and west coasts. Point out the importance of geography—mountains, rivers, deserts, and the plains—in choosing their routes. Have groups present their routes and explain the thinking.

Advertisements

The Central Pacific and Union Pacific railroads needed workers to build the railroads, and then they needed passengers to fill their trains. Ask students to create advertisements placed by the railroads for workers or passengers. Remind them to think about the qualities a worker should have and/or what the railroads could offer their passengers. As an alternate assignment, students can design an invitation to the ceremony at Promontory Summit in Utah on May 10, 1869.

Other Transportation Firsts

A trip on the transcontinental railroad from Omaha to Sacramento was scheduled to take 4 days, 4 hours, and 40 minutes. A first-class ticket cost $111.00, a second-class ticket cost $80, and a third-class ticket was $40. Which other transportation firsts do students think affected American lives? Based on their research, create a class timeline of these events.

10 Easy-to-Read American History Plays • Scholastic Professional Books © 2001

ELLIS ISLAND AND ANGEL ISLAND

Immigration (1892-1910)

Cast of Characters (in order of appearance)

at Ellis Island

Sasha Bernstein: *Twelve-year-old Russian Jewish girl*

Marty Bernstein: *Sasha's younger brother*

Solomon Bernstein: *Sasha and Marty's father*

Irina Bernstein: *Sasha and Marty's mother*

Ruth Kokernot: *Russian Jewish woman*

Mr. Hopson: *Ellis Island inspector*

at Angel Island

Mr. Wayne: *Inspector*

Paul Gee: *Fourteen-year-old Chinese boy*

Tet Kwan: *Chinese man*

Richard Sing: *Chinese man*

10 Easy-to-Read American History Plays • Scholastic Professional Books © 2001

ACT 1 • Ellis Island, New York (1892)

SASHA BERNSTEIN: Look at all the people! I've never seen so many people in one place before!

MARTY BERNSTEIN: I can't understand what anybody but us is saying. Everybody's speaking different languages. Where do we go? What do we do?

SOLOMON BERNSTEIN: Follow them. They look like they know what they're doing.

IRINA BERNSTEIN *(raising her voice)*: Is anybody from Russia? Does anybody speak Yiddish?

RUTH KOKERNOT: I do. And you shouldn't follow those people. The doctor has already looked at them. See the letters in chalk on their sleeves? *E* means eye disease. *H* means heart problems. They may get sent back to where they came from.

SASHA BERNSTEIN: We won't get sent back. We're healthy.

SOLOMON BERNSTEIN: We were healthy when we left Russia—in the middle of the night, with the clothes on our backs and a little food. Then we walked for a week into Germany to catch the steamship. Then we finally got on a ship—

RUTH KOKERNOT: Don't tell me. I know. There was no room. The food was terrible, and there wasn't much of it. The water was bad, and there wasn't much of it, either.

IRINA BERNSTEIN: We *were* healthy when we left Russia.

SOLOMON BERNSTEIN: We're lucky we are even *alive*. The czar's soldiers came riding into our village. We were lucky to escape.

RUTH KOKERNOT: I know. I saw terrible things, terrible things—so many of us hurt and killed, because we're Jewish.

SASHA BERNSTEIN: Which line do we get in? We want to get out of here and go into New York City.

RUTH KOKERNOT: First the doctor has to look at you. You stand in that line. Then, if you don't get anything marked in chalk on your sleeve, you get in that line over there. How much money do you have?

SOLOMON BERNSTEIN: What?

RUTH KOKERNOT: You have to have at least twenty-five dollars or they won't let you in. You have to have a place to stay. You have to have a job.

IRINA BERNSTEIN: We have to have twenty-five dollars? Nobody told us that. The boat tickets took almost all the money we had.

MARTY BERNSTEIN: We have a place to stay! My uncle Theo found an apartment for us. Papa and I are going to work in the garment factory where he works.

SASHA BERNSTEIN: Mama and I are going to work at home, sewing clothes.

SOLOMON BERNSTEIN: We don't have twenty-five dollars.

RUTH KOKERNOT: How much do you have?

SOLOMON BERNSTEIN: It looks like . . . almost twenty dollars.

RUTH KOKERNOT: That's not enough.

IRINA BERNSTEIN: But it's almost enough.

RUTH KOKERNOT: Here—here's five dollars.

SOLOMON BERNSTEIN: We can't take your money.

RUTH KOKERNOT: Look, do you want to get sent back to Russia? You've got jobs. You can pay me back.

MR. HOPSON: Keep it moving, keep it moving. We don't have all day. *(to Solomon)* What's your name?

SOLOMON BERNSTEIN: What?

RUTH KOKERNOT: He wants to know what your name is.

SOLOMON BERNSTEIN: Oh. Solomon Bernstein, and this is my wife Irina—

MR. HOPSON: Sal Burns and Irene Burns. Welcome to America. Get in that line over there.

SOLOMON BERNSTEIN: No, no, my name is Solomon Bernstein—

RUTH KOKERNOT: That's not your name anymore, Sal. Welcome to America.

➤ ACT 2 • Angel Island, California (1910) ➤

SCENE 1: AN OFFICE AT ANGEL ISLAND

MR. WAYNE: Okay, Paul Gee. Sit down. Take it easy. Just answer my questions, and you'll get out of here.

PAUL GEE: Thank you.

MR. WAYNE: First question—are you here all by yourself?

PAUL GEE: My father is waiting for me in San Francisco.

MR. WAYNE: You'll live with your father?

PAUL GEE: Yes, sir.

MR. WAYNE: You're not a paper son, are you?

10 Easy-to-Read American History Plays • Scholastic Professional Books © 2001

PAUL GEE: Excuse me?

MR. WAYNE: You're not pretending to be someone's son—someone who just happens to be an American citizen already? You're not paying someone to say that you're his son?

PAUL GEE: No, sir! He really is my father. We look just like each other, too. If you saw him, you would know that he's my father.

MR. WAYNE: I'm sure. Let's talk a little bit about China. How many brothers and sisters do you have?

PAUL GEE: I have two sisters and two brothers.

MR. WAYNE: Okay. How many windows are there in your house?

PAUL GEE: There are six windows in my house.

MR. WAYNE: I'm sure. Where is your house located in the village?

PAUL GEE: My house . . . in the village . . . it's . . . one, two, three, four—fourth house in the second row.

MR. WAYNE: Is that your final answer?

PAUL GEE: Yes, sir. My house is the fourth house in the second row.

MR. WAYNE: Who lives in the second house in the fourth row?

PAUL GEE: The second house in the fourth row? Hmmm . . . Gong Zhou lives there.

MR. WAYNE: All by himself?

PAUL GEE: No, sir—all by herself. Her husband died last winter. They had no children.

MR. WAYNE: What did her husband die from?

PAUL GEE: He was very sick. He coughed a lot. Excuse me, sir?

MR. WAYNE: What?

PAUL GEE: Why are you asking me so many questions? Why does it matter how many windows my house in China has?

MR. WAYNE: I have to make sure you are who you say you are. You could be making all this up just to get in to the United States. You could be thinking that you'll get rich quick here by taking jobs from real Americans. Then you'll take all your money back to China.

PAUL GEE: Oh, no, sir. I mean, I will work hard here. I want to become an American citizen.

MR. WAYNE: I'll tell you this—you'll either get to go to San Francisco in about a month, or you'll get sent back to China.

10 Easy-to-Read American History Plays • Scholastic Professional Books © 2001

PAUL GEE: Why would you send me back?

MR. WAYNE: If we find out that you lied to us, we'll send you back. Your house better be the second house in the fourth row.

PAUL GEE: Excuse me, sir. It's the fourth house in the second row.

MR. WAYNE: We'll see about that.

SCENE 2: A FEW WEEKS LATER

TET KWAN: Don't worry, Paul. You haven't even been here for a month.

RICHARD SING: He's right. I've been here for almost two months.

PAUL GEE: But my father said they would keep me here at Angel Island for a week or two.

TET KWAN: Don't worry. You'll be out of here before you know it.

RICHARD SING: He's right. Why don't you go play some volleyball? It'll make the time go by faster.

PAUL GEE: I guess you're right.

(Paul leaves.)

TET KWAN: I hope he gave the right answers to all the questions. I hope they let him go to San Francisco.

RICHARD SING: I hope they let us *all* go to San Francisco.

(Mr. Wayne walks in. Paul follows him.)

MR. WAYNE: I've got some good news and some bad news. Listen up. Richard Sing— San Francisco! Ho Chin—back to Hong Kong! Paul Gee—San Francisco!

PAUL GEE: I made it! I made it!

TET KWAN: See, everything turned out all right.

PAUL GEE: But what about you? He didn't call your name.

TET KWAN: At least I'm not being sent back to China. I'm still in America. Richard, take care of Paul. Make sure he finds his father.

RICHARD SING: We'll see you when you get to San Francisco, Tet. It won't be long, maybe tomorrow even.

(They all shake hands. Paul and Richard leave.)

TET KWAN: Maybe tomorrow, maybe never.

10 Easy-to-Read American History Plays • Scholastic Professional Books © 2001

TEACHING GUIDE

Background

Between 1892 and 1920, over 23 million immigrants to the United States were processed at Ellis Island. Its opening coincided with the second great wave of immigration from Southern and Eastern Europe that began in the 1880s. The immigrants were first examined by doctors. If they were deemed unhealthy, they could be sent back to their originating countries; families were often separated in this way. About 2 percent of the immigrants who had contagious diseases or couldn't take care of themselves were sent back. Healthy immigrants were then questioned by inspectors. At this stage, names were often changed—shortened or misspelled by the inspectors. Immigrants also had to have at least twenty-five dollars, the promise of jobs, and places to stay. After leaving Ellis Island, immigrants either remained in New York City or traveled by train to other destinations—Boston, Philadelphia, Baltimore, and the Midwest. In 1921, after Congress passed restrictive quotas on European immigration, Ellis Island was used for the purposes of detaining and deporting aliens. It was closed in 1954.

Angel Island was expected to become the "Ellis Island of the West" after the Panama Canal was opened. World War I interfered, however, and the majority of immigrants passing through its doors were from Asia. The first Chinese immigrants to the United States arrived in 1848, and more followed, primarily to work the California gold fields. Severe unemployment in the 1870s led to discrimination against the Chinese and led to restrictions against Asian immigration. Only those who had been born in the United States, or had husbands or fathers who were citizens, could enter the country. The San Francisco earthquake destroyed records, so citizenship was often difficult to prove. Thousands of "paper sons" and "paper daughters" claiming to be the real sons and daughters of Chinese-American citizens entered the country. Immigrants were held at Angel Island anywhere from two weeks to two years. Inspectors asked detailed questions about the Chinese immigrants' home villages. Those who didn't pass the questioning were sent back to China. Many of the detainees wrote poetry on the wooden walls while they waited to hear their fate. Angel Island closed on November 5, 1940.

Both Ellis Island and Angel Island, once abandoned, are now museums.

Vocabulary   Some readers may not be familiar with the following words:

citizen: person who is born in a country, or who becomes a member of that country by law

czar: ruler (king) in Russia before 1917

garment: piece of clothing

immigration: the act of coming to a new country to live

inspector: person who looks at someone or something

Yiddish: language spoken by many European Jews

Books to Build Interest

The Chinese-American Experience (Coming to America) by Dana Ying-Hui Wu (Millbrook, 1993)

I Was Dreaming to Come to America: Memories from the Ellis Island Oral History Project (Puffin, 1997)

If Your Name Was Changed at Ellis Island by Ellen Levine (Scholastic, 1994)

Web Sites

http://angel-island.com (Oral histories and photographs of Angel Island)

http://angelisland.org (Angel Island Association)

http://ellisisland.com (Ellis Island Immigration Museum)

10 Easy-to-Read American History Plays • Scholastic Professional Books © 2001

ACTIVITIES

Family Tree

Besides Ellis Island and Angel Island, immigrants entered the United States through other port cities such as Boston, New Orleans, and Galveston, Texas. Many stayed in those cities, but others traveled inland. How did your students get where they are today? Have them interview family members so they can use oral histories to make their own family trees. A useful book to help students get started is Lila Perl's *The Great Ancestor Hunt* (Houghton Mifflin, 1991).

From ?? to the United States

Immigrants usually come to the United States for economic, political, or social reasons. Often, the events in their home countries—drought, political upheaval, religious persecution—forced people to leave and seek better lives elsewhere. Have students choose one country and explore its pattern of immigration to the United States. They may present a straightforward report with graphs and charts, or a fictionalized account of one person's story in the form of a diary or a play. Encourage them to create a map that shows the route that an immigrant from that country might take.

Angel Island Poetry

An Asian immigrant could be detained at Angel Island anywhere from two weeks to two years. Often, detainees wrote or carved poems into the walls at Angel Island, some of which can still be seen today. These poems can be found in the book *Island: Poetry and History of Asian Immigration on Angel Island 1910–1940* by Him Mark Lai, Judy Yung, and Genny Lim (University of Washington Press, 1997). Share the book with students, and encourage them to write their own poems on topics such as moving to a new place, immigration to America, or what living in the United States means to them.

History of Ellis Island and Angel Island

After being closed to immigration, both Ellis Island and Angel Island fell into disrepair and were almost forgotten. Now visitors can take a ferry to Ellis Island and stand in the Great Hall where immigrants were processed. They can also go to Angel Island and see the poetry carved into the walls. Ask students to research the history of Ellis Island or Angel Island—before, during, and after they served as immigration stations.

Communicating Without Words

Immigrants from many different countries poured into Ellis Island. An inspector or doctor couldn't hope to communicate with each immigrant in his or her language; immigrants from different countries, or even different regions of the same country, couldn't speak to each other. Challenge students to think about how they would communicate with someone who spoke a different and unfamiliar language. Then set aside a portion of time for them, and you, to communicate without using words. After the experiment, talk about the experience. Which forms of communication—pantomime, drawing, for instance—worked the best? What did students find rewarding and frustrating about the experiment?

Immigration to Your Community

What is the story of immigration to your community? When was it founded, and by whom? How has the population changed over the years? If possible, enlist the aid of the local historical society or school or public librarian to help students find out more about immigration to their community. Consider having them collaborate on a play or series of skits about the changes in their community.

10 Easy-to-Read American History Plays • Scholastic Professional Books © 2001